CAREER GUIDANCE FOR TEENS MADE SIMPLE

IDENTIFY YOUR PASSION, IMPROVE ESSENTIAL SKILLS, REFINE JOB-SEEKING TECHNIQUES AND LAND YOUR DREAM JOB!

H. L. CARLISLE

TABLE OF CONTENTS

INTRODUCTION

"I mean, everyone talks about the future, but I have no clue where to start," Emily, her fingers absently tracing patterns on the bleacher surface, looks up at the Washington High football field before them. Her classmates were enthusiastically participating in gym class activities below, but Emily couldn't have felt more alone.

Alex, leaning back on his palms and gazing at the blue sky, nods in agreement. "Yeah, it's like we're supposed to have it all figured out, but I feel completely lost," he said.

"Yeah," Emily said, twirling a strand of dark hair around one of her fingers. "I don't get why we're supposed to have our whole lives figured out now. It's so much pressure."

Alex, picking at his shoelace, nods in agreement. "Right? And what if we choose the wrong thing? We're stuck with it for, like, forever."

As their fellow Senior class laughs and runs around on the field below them, Emily can't help but frown.

"I don't want a job that, like, makes me sacrifice who I am, you know? But it feels like we might have just to make everyone else happy," Emily confides.

"There are so many options for jobs. I mean, it's super scary. How do we even know where to start?" Alex asks, eyebrows furrowed.

"It's like we're entering this whole new world, and I don't feel ready for it," Emily admits, her voice tinged with apprehension.

"I mean, just look," Alex gestures to his classmates, "I see people who know exactly what they want to do, and I'm here, still figuring it out. It's frustrating," Alex adds.

"Yo, guys!"

Emily and Alex turn to see a girl with a blonde braid climbing up the bleachers toward them, each step echoing on the metal stairs.

"Hey, Lily," Alex greeted her.

"I couldn't help but overhear your conversation," she says, offering a warm smile and sitting down next to them. "I get it. Figuring out the whole career thing is like trying to solve a massive puzzle without all the pieces."

"Tell me 'bout it," Emily huffs, resting her chin in her hand.

"Get this, though," I just read this book and I learned about this new way of looking at things."

"What do you mean?" Alex said, tilting his head to the side.

"It's this thing called the 'Seeing Strategy'. It's this approach to navigating the craziness," she begins.

Emily leans back and crosses her arms. "Go on."

"Well, the first step is 'Serving Yourself'," Lily emphasizes, "is all about boosting confidence, practicing self-care, and embracing mindfulness. It's like laying the foundation for everything else."

"Hmm. That sounds nice," Alex ponders, absorbing the wisdom.

"Right?" Lily continues, "And then next is, Excelling Academically. It involves mastering time management, efficient studying, and exploring your interests. It's about making your education work for you, not the other way around."

"That's the dream," Emily comments. "What's after that?"

"Exploring Interests," she smiles, "is where the fun begins. Hobbies, extracurriculars – they're not just pastimes. They're avenues for discovering what sets your soul on fire."

"Okay, bet," Alex says, imagining that coming to reality.

"Then, in the 'Impacts of Community,' you find your people," Lily adds. "Building a support network, navigating social situations... it's crucial for growth."

"Kinda like we have each other, right?" Emily jokes, nudging Alex in the shoulder.

As the two laugh, Lily goes on to explain the next step. "You see, then we go on to Navigating New Experiences," she says with enthusiasm, "This one is about stepping out of your comfort zone. Gain experiences, take steps toward a career. Don't be afraid to dive into the unknown."

Finally, Lily concludes with 'Going the Distance.' She tells her friends that, "Life's a marathon, not a sprint. Resilience and adaptability... These will keep you focused on the long-term purpose."

The three friends sit a little taller, absorbing Lily's words.

"And trust me," she winks, "I've got plenty more tips where these came from. We'll tackle this together."

The football field, once a source of uncertainty, now becomes a space for shared understanding and newfound purpose.

* * *

Emily and Alex are not alone in their fears. Many teens, all around the world, go through these same worries. For that reason, I invite you to embark on a transformative journey through the pages of this book. It's more than just a collection of words; it's a personalized guide to shortcuts that will redefine the way you approach life's challenges. This book unfolds as a beacon of wisdom, shedding light on the intricate path of career choices and personal development.

Within these pages, you'll encounter the "Seeing Strategy," a holistic approach that empowers you on various fronts. *Serving yourself* becomes a sanctuary for raising confidence, nurturing self-esteem, and embracing self-care and mindfulness. *Excelling academically* unveils tips for mastering time management, studying efficiently, and delving into your interests. *Exploring interests* becomes a journey of self-discovery, where hobbies and extracurricular activities transform into avenues for gaining valuable skills. *Impacts of community* guide you in finding a supportive network and navigating social situations with finesse. *Navigating new experiences* propels you forward, encouraging hands-on learning and decisive steps toward a meaningful career. *Going the distance* instills the importance of resilience and adaptability, laying the foundation for enduring purpose.

Imagine the results awaiting you... a life where you confidently navigate the complexities of academia, excel in your studies, explore your passions, and build meaningful connections. This book is your personalized roadmap to a future marked by success, purpose, and fulfillment.

Before this guidance, your journey was marked by uncertainties about career choices, academic pressures, and the fear of failure. The new information will act as a guiding light, offering once elusive insights. Reflect on the difficulties you faced without this guidance, and witness the transformative potential that awaits.

As we move ahead, consider this journey as an engaging conversation, a casual exchange of ideas. Imagine turning the pages of this guide as if we're embarking on an exploration together. We've set the foundation, and now it's time to zoom in on what sets you apart. The upcoming chapter serves as a compass, guiding you to recognize your strengths, quirks, and the elements that define you. It's not just about self-awareness; it's about unlocking doors to a realm of possibilities.

WHO ARE YOU?

> *Your work is going to fill a large part of your life, and the only way to be truly satisfied is to do what you believe is great work. And the only way to do great work is to love what you do.*

— STEVE JOBS

"You know, sometimes I feel like I don't really know who I am," Emily admits. She takes the rock in her hand and tosses it against the shimmering surface of the lake. "It's like I'm wandering in this maze, and I'm not sure where I'm headed."

Alex and Lily exchange a glance. Then Alex, with a knowing smile, skips a stone effortlessly, its brief dance on the water mirroring the complexities of their shared conversation.

"You're not alone, Emily. We all go through moments of uncertainty. It's like trying to navigate a path in a dense forest, not always sure which direction to take."

Lily, observing the ripples created by Alex's well-aimed stone, adds, "I get it. Life can feel like a puzzle with missing pieces. But you know, sometimes the most beautiful pictures come together with time."

"I guess. Sometimes, though, it really gets to me," Emily says.

Lily turns to her friend and says, "You know, guys, Steve Jobs once said, 'Your work is going to fill a large part of your life, and the only way to be truly satisfied is to do what you believe is great work. And the only way to do great work is to love what you do.'"

The words hang in the air.

Alex, still skimming stones, pauses to absorb the wisdom.

Lily continues, "I think what Steve Jobs meant is that finding satisfaction in what you do is key to a fulfilling life. If we love what we're doing, it becomes more than just a job; it becomes a passion, a journey. It's like skipping stones… you find the right rhythm, and each skip feels purposeful."

Emily, thoughtful, watches Lily's stone create intricate ripples on the water's surface. Lily elaborates, "When we align our work with our passions and beliefs, it's not just a means to an end. It becomes a part of who we are. That way, even when we feel lost, our love for what we do can guide us back to our path, just like these stones finding their way across the lake."

The trio, connected by the shared experience and the profound words of Steve Jobs, continues to skip stones, finding solace in the idea that, in the journey of self-discovery, embracing what you love can lead to a more satisfying and purposeful life.

* * *

Emily finds herself navigating a common challenge among teenagers...the uncertainty of determining their life path when self-identity remains elusive. It's a shared struggle because, let's be real, decoding oneself is a complex task.

Our mission now is to unravel this intricacy together. We'll delve into recognizing strengths, acknowledging our interests, and comprehending the elements that define us as individuals. Why embark on this journey? Well, understanding ourselves is akin to possessing a compass, guiding us toward careers that align with our true selves.

So, buckle up! We're embarking on a journey of self-discovery. The goal is for each one of us to be closer to unraveling the enigma. Ready for this expedition? Let's delve into it with determination.

WHAT DEFINES YOU?

Getting to know yourself is like having your guide on this journey to finding a career that really fits. Think of it as having a GPS for navigating the twists and turns of life choices and work adventures. Figuring out who you are is super important when it comes to building a satisfying career, and it all boils down to three key things: your values, interests, and skills.

Understanding your values is like figuring out your moral compass, it helps you make decisions that feel right. When picking a career, matching up your professional choices with your personal values gives your work a sense of purpose and authenticity. If your job aligns with what you believe in, it not only makes you happy at work but also adds a positive vibe to your whole life. Recognizing and living by your values means you're less likely to feel conflicted or unsure about your career path, making it more meaningful and rewarding.

Digging into your interests is like going on a self-discovery adventure to find what really excites you. Choosing a career that lines up with your interests turns work from a chore into something you genuinely enjoy. When your job connects with your passion, it brings out your creativity and keeps your curiosity alive. Adding your interests to your career not only boosts job satisfaction but also keeps you learning and growing.

Skills, both the technical and people kind, are like your toolset for any job. Knowing your skills is key to figuring out where you excel. A career that lets you use and build on your skills makes you really good at what you do and gives you a sense of accomplishment. Understanding your skills helps you make smart career choices, guiding you toward roles that match your strengths and offer chances for even more growth.

So, finding the right career is basically a journey into the core of who you are. It's about understanding your values to guide your choices, discovering interests that fuel your passion, and recognizing skills that make you awesome at what you do. Knowing yourself in these ways not only increases the chances of picking a career that feels right but also adds balance, purpose, and satisfaction to your life journey. It's like having a guide that points you towards careers that match your true self, bringing a deep sense of fulfillment and accomplishment.

KNOW YOUR VALUES

Value:
(noun)
The beliefs people have, especially about what is right and wrong and what is most important in life, that control their behavior.

Understanding your values is a crucial part of navigating life, making decisions, and figuring out who you are. In simple terms, values are like the compass that guides your actions, showing you what you believe is right or wrong. In the article, *Values*, found on "Ethics Unwrapped", we learn that values are society's shared beliefs about what is good or bad and how people should act.

The passage emphasizes that values often come from the environment you grew up in, and you might consider them "right" because they are the values of your particular culture. It points out that when it comes to making ethical decisions, you often have to weigh different values against each other. This can be tricky, especially when people have different values, leading to conflicting preferences and priorities.

The article categorizes values into different types. There are those with intrinsic worth, like love, truth, and freedom... things that are universally considered valuable. Then there are values like ambition, responsibility, and courage, which describe traits or behaviors that are useful means to an end, like achieving a goal.

The passage also touches on sacred values, which are seen as moral imperatives for those who believe in them. These values are not easily compromised because they are viewed as duties rather than just factors to consider in decision-making. It acknowledges that values can vary from person to person and across cultures and time but emphasizes that they play a universal role in ethical decision-making.

So, in a nutshell, knowing your values helps you understand what truly matters to you, guides your actions, and contributes to making ethical decisions in your life. It's like having a personal guide that helps you stay true to yourself, even when faced with tough choices.

Examples of Values
How Workplaces Can Support or Conflict with Them:

- Value: Diversity and Inclusion
  - Supportive Jobs: Diversity and Inclusion Specialist, Human Resources Manager focusing on inclusive hiring practices
  - Conflicting Jobs: Workplace with discriminatory policies, organizations lacking diversity initiatives

- Value: Work-Life Balance
  - Supportive Jobs: Flexible remote work positions, companies with emphasis on employee well-being
  - Conflicting Jobs: High-pressure investment banking jobs with excessive overtime requirements

- Value: Social Responsibility
  - Supportive Jobs: Nonprofit roles, Corporate Social Responsibility (CSR) Manager
  - Conflicting Jobs: Tobacco industry executive, positions with a history of unethical business practices

- Value: Continuous Learning and Growth
  - Supportive Jobs: Research scientist, roles in dynamic industries with opportunities for skill development
  - Conflicting Jobs: Repetitive, stagnant roles with limited opportunities for advancement

- Value: Innovation and Creativity
  - Supportive Jobs: Product designer, tech startup roles
  - Conflicting Jobs: Bureaucratic environments with resistance to change, jobs with rigid processes

- Value: Health and Well-being
  - Supportive Jobs: Wellness coach, healthcare professional
  - Conflicting Jobs: Stressful high-demand positions, industries with poor occupational safety standards

COGNITIVE DISSONANCE

Once you understand your values and how that impacts your choice of career, another important concept to think about is cognitive dissonance.

Ever heard of cognitive dissonance? It's like when your actions or decisions don't quite match up with your values and it can mess with your head.

Let's break it down.

Imagine you're all about environmental sustainability, right? You recycle, you avoid single-use plastic... you're a green champion. Now, picture landing a job at a company that's not so eco-friendly. That clash between your values and the company's practices? That's cognitive dissonance.

Now, how does this relate to job satisfaction and your overall well-being? Well, when you're stuck in a job that doesn't align with your values, it's like wearing shoes that don't fit. Uncomfortable, right?

Let's say you're passionate about creativity, but your job involves repetitive tasks with zero room for imagination. That dissonance can leave you feeling unsatisfied and, over time, kinda miserable.

Another example: you value work-life balance, but your job demands crazy overtime. It's like a seesaw tipping too much to one side. That imbalance messes with your happiness and can even affect your mental health.

Cognitive dissonance isn't just a fancy term; it's a real challenge. It can make you question your choices, feel stressed, and impact your overall well-being. So, it's crucial to recognize it and, if possible, make changes to align your values with your actions. After all, life's too short to be stuck in a job that doesn't vibe with who you are.

Values aren't just these abstract ideas floating around.

They should show up in what you do, how you decide things, and how you act. When your actions line up with your values, it's like skipping the perfect stone... you feel that rush of satisfaction and authenticity. Remember, values inform action, and that's the key to living your best, most authentic life.

In her article, *Values, Passion, or Purpose — Which Should Guide Your Career?* Irina Cozma emphasizes these ideas. She asserts that "values are not just abstract concepts — they should manifest in your actions, decisions, and behaviors. When your values are in alignment with your actions, you will experience greater satisfaction and authenticity." This is the reason that values can help you navigate the twists and turns of life, especially when it comes to making career choices.

KNOW YOUR INTERESTS

Interest:

(noun)

The feeling of wanting to give your attention to something or of wanting to be involved with and to discover more about something.

Passion and purpose often go hand in hand, creating a dynamic blend that propels us towards meaningful endeavors. Passion, marked by intense enthusiasm, and purpose, providing a sense of direction and contribution, intertwine to give our actions a deeper significance. When we're passionate about something, whether a cause or an activity, we naturally find purpose in it, extending beyond personal satisfaction. This intersection becomes a driving force, motivating us to overcome challenges, make a positive impact, and discover fulfillment in our pursuits. As we delve into the realm of interest, it's essential to acknowledge how the convergence of passion and purpose shapes our journey and leads us to truly rewarding experiences.

Understanding what you're into is super important because it plays a big part in shaping who you are, influencing your choices, and even affecting how you feel overall. In simpler terms, interests are the things you really like or are drawn to—stuff that gets you excited, happy, or even fired up. Figuring out and accepting what you're into can give you direction and motivation in different parts of your life.

In his article, *Passion: Definition, Examples, & Projects,* Charlie Huntington makes a big deal about interests, saying, "being passionate is crucial for feeling fulfilled and finding personal meaning; it's a key part of being your best self." This basically means that interests, which are a part of passion, help a lot in reaching your full potential and feeling complete as a person.

Checking out your interests isn't just about having fun with certain activities; it goes deeper. Huntington believes that "passions usually have a strong emotional component. If you are interested in something but do not feel strongly about it, whether good or bad, then you are probably not passionate about it." This points out that interests aren't just random likes; they're tied to your emotions, making them pretty powerful in shaping how you see and experience things.

Huntington gets into why we get passionate, talking about the "Self-Determination Theory". It suggests that people develop passions by doing things that fulfill their basic needs like wanting to be independent, feeling capable, and connecting with others.Huntington thinks that we "achieve self-determination by interacting with our environments to achieve these goals," basically meaning that interests are a big part of figuring out who you are and growing as a person.

Understanding your interests can lead to a more fulfilling life. Huntington thinks that "with more passion in their lives people tend to have better mental and physical well-being." This backs up the idea that doing things you're into is good for your overall health and happiness. This connection between interests and well-being shows how exploring and embracing your passions can seriously boost your satisfaction with life.

To sum it up, knowing what you're into is crucial for growing as a person, feeling fulfilled, and just being well overall. The deep emotions tied to interests, their role in making you independent and capable, and the positive effect they have on your mental and physical health all highlight how important it is to understand and embrace your unique interests.

Examples of Interests to be Passionate About
• Environmental Sustainability: Teens passionate about the environment might explore careers in environmental science, conservation, sustainable agriculture, or renewable energy.
• Technology and Coding: Those interested in technology and coding may pursue careers in software development, cybersecurity, or artificial intelligence.
• Animal Rights: Teens passionate about animal rights might consider careers as veterinarians, animal welfare advocates, or wildlife conservationists.
• Health and Wellness: Interests in health and wellness could lead to careers in nursing, nutrition, physical therapy, or personal training.
• Arts and Creativity: Teens with a flair for creativity might explore careers in graphic design, filmmaking, writing, or performing arts.
• Social Justice and Activism: Those passionate about social justice and activism may pursue careers in law, community organizing, or advocacy for marginalized communities.
• Science and Research: Teens interested in science may consider careers in research, biology, chemistry, or physics.
• Culinary Arts: Passion for cooking and culinary arts could lead to careers as chefs, nutritionists, or food bloggers.
• Sports: Teens who love sports might explore careers as athletes, sports analysts, physical therapists, or sports journalists.
• Fashion and Design: Interests in fashion and design could lead to careers as fashion designers, stylists, or textile engineers.
• Travel and Exploration: Those passionate about travel might consider careers in tourism, international relations, or journalism focused on travel.
• History and Humanities: Teens interested in history and humanities may pursue careers in museum curation, historical research, or archaeology.
• STEM Fields: Passion for science, technology, engineering, and mathematics (STEM) may lead to careers in engineering, computer science, or mathematics research.
• Music and Performing Arts: Teens with a love for music and performing arts might consider careers as musicians, actors, or music producers.
• Psychology and Mental Health: Interests in psychology and mental health could lead to careers as psychologists, counselors, or psychiatrists.

Journey to Joy: Pursuing Interests for a Satisfying Work-Life

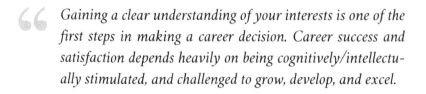

Gaining a clear understanding of your interests is one of the first steps in making a career decision. Career success and satisfaction depends heavily on being cognitively/intellectually stimulated, and challenged to grow, develop, and excel.

— JAMES COOK UNIVERSITY

A sense of purpose, of *passion*, is important to achieve success and fulfillment. In his article, *The Definitions of Purpose, Passion, and Vision*, Bill Davis captures the essence of pursuing interests for satisfaction in work by stating, "Your passions are your internal energy source, the fire or determination you have for reaching some destination up ahead. They tell you why you are on this journey and what you want from life. They are your push and pull." This quote encapsulates the idea that passions serve as a driving force, guiding individuals on their life journey and influencing their desires. When individuals align their interests with their work, it becomes a powerful source of internal motivation. Pursuing interests not only adds meaning to one's professional life but also fuels determination and commitment.

Here are key points emphasizing the importance of pursuing interests for fulfillment and satisfaction in work:

- **Intrinsic Motivation:** Interests and passions serve as intrinsic motivators. When individuals engage in work aligned with their interests, they tap into a natural source of enthusiasm, contributing to a more fulfilling and satisfying work experience.
- **Guiding Life and Career Decisions:** Identifying and pursuing one's interests help shape goals, guide career decisions, and provide a sense of direction. This intentional alignment leads to a more purposeful and meaningful career path.
- **Energy Source for Success:** Interests act as an internal energy source, igniting the determination and resilience needed to overcome challenges. This passion becomes the

driving force propelling individuals toward their desired destinations.

- **Visionary Perspective:** Integrating personal interests into one's career vision allows for a holistic and long-term perspective. A vision influenced by genuine passions can motivate individuals to make a positive impact on their work and the world.
- **Achieving Work-Life Balance:** Balancing work and personal interests is crucial for maintaining overall well-being. Spending time on activities that align with personal passions contributes to a more balanced and satisfying life.
- Positive Outcomes: Pursuing interests can lead to positive outcomes, fostering a sense of achievement and growth. Visualizing future success, as recommended in the article, becomes more attainable when fueled by genuine passions.

The journey toward fulfillment and satisfaction in work involves recognizing, embracing, and integrating personal interests into one's professional life. The internal energy derived from pursuing passions propels individuals toward success and adds depth and purpose to their careers.

KNOW YOUR SKILLS

Skill:
(noun)
The ability to use one's knowledge effectively and readily in execution or performance.

Knowing your skills is crucial because they are like your super-powers, helping you navigate through life and reach success in whatever you choose to do. Indeed's editorial team describes what skills are in their article, *What Are Skills? (With Tips on How to Improve Them)*. The authors explain that they are not just things you're born with; they're abilities you develop through experiences and learning. They come in different types, and everyone has a unique set.

There are many different categories of skills such as job skills, leadership skills, business intelligence skills, organizational skills, and life skills. Each type plays a role in shaping how you handle tasks, work with others, and achieve your goals. Indeed explains that "skill is a term that encompasses the knowledge, competencies, and abilities to perform operational tasks." This means that your skills are like tools in a toolbox, helping you tackle challenges and get things done. They can be learned and improved over time, making them valuable assets in various areas of your life.

Skills can be measured and tested, making them a reliable way for employers to understand what you bring to the table. Indeed states, "Most jobs require multiple skills, and likewise, some skills will be more useful for certain professions than others." So, by knowing your skills, you can tailor your choices to match what you're good at and what you enjoy doing.

Improving your skills will provide monumental benefits in both your professional and personal life. It's like leveling up in a game… the better your skills, the more opportunities open up for you. Once you identify your skills, you need to go through many steps such as setting goals, getting support, and having fun with the process. You need to show that improving your skills is not just about work; it's a journey of growth and self-discovery.

So, understanding your skills is like unlocking your potential. As Indeed says, "Improving your skills can open new doors to better opportunities." It's about recognizing your strengths, honing them, and using them to create a path to success that is uniquely yours.

Hard Skills

 Hard skills are easy to quantify – they are the technical knowledge you learn either in the classroom or on the job, and you prove them through certifications, degrees or other qualifications.

— DEAKIN UNIVERSITY

Hard skills are like the special tools that you pick up through school, work, or other training experiences. They're the technical abilities you need to do specific tasks, and jobs often mention them directly in descriptions. The Indeed Editorial Team describes hard skills as the "technical knowledge or training that you have gained through any life experience, including in your career or education." These skills can be anything from speaking multiple languages, being a computer whiz, or even knowing how to use software like Microsoft Excel. Imagine you're aiming to become an architect... you'd need to learn how to use drafting software and get the necessary license to practice. You can gain hard skills in different ways, like going to college or taking courses, getting hands-on experience at work, or even volunteering. Essentially, it's about learning and mastering the specific tools you'll need for the job you want.

Examples of Hard Skills
• Programming languages (e.g., Python, Java, Ruby)
• Database management
• Bilingual or multilingual proficiency
• Adobe software suite proficiency
• Network security knowledge
• SEO/SEM marketing expertise
• Statistical analysis
• Data mining
• Mobile development skills
• User interface design
• Marketing campaign management
• Proficiency in specific programming languages (e.g., Perl)
• Technical proficiency in areas like computer programming and coding
• Editing skills, such as video or written content editing
• Knowledge of storage systems and management

Getting good at hard skills involves picking up know-how from different places, and it's not as complicated as it might sound. If you're more of a classroom person, hitting up university or college is a classic move. You get the book smarts and hands-on practice. For those who prefer one-on-one learning, private lessons are a cool option. They're like your personal skill boosters. Taking specific courses or grabbing certificates, online or offline, is a quick and recognized way to build up those hard skills. Once you're out there in the working world, actual job experiences kick in - you learn by doing. And hey, don't underestimate the power of volunteering. You get to help out while snagging some practical skills. So, whether you're in a classroom, learning one-on-one, taking online courses, working, or giving back, these paths are like your skill-building toolbox, making you a well-rounded pro in no time.

Soft Skills

Soft skills—also known as "people skills" or "interpersonal skills"—are a set of personal attributes and abilities that allow individuals to effectively interact with others in a professional setting. At their core, these include the ability to collaborate effectively, manage time, and communicate with clarity, among others.

— MONIQUE DANAO

In today's fast-paced world, landing success at work isn't just about technical know-how; it's also about having essential soft skills that help you navigate the professional landscape. Soft skills, often called "people skills," are personal qualities crucial for thriving in a work setting. They include things like being a good communicator, showing leadership, working well in a team, and being creative. For instance, effective communication is not just about talking; it's also about understanding others and expressing your thoughts clearly. Being a leader means inspiring your team and setting clear goals. Teamwork is about working together with others toward a common objective, fostering creativity and innovation. Creativity involves thinking outside the box and coming up with new ideas. These soft skills are important in various industries, making them valuable for success at work.

Examples of Soft Skills
• Communication: The ability to express ideas clearly and listen actively, fostering strong interpersonal relationships.
• Leadership: Inspiring and guiding others towards common goals, taking initiative, and making sound decisions.
• Teamwork: Collaborating effectively with others, contributing to group objectives, and valuing diverse perspectives.
• Creativity: Thinking outside the box, generating innovative ideas, and approaching challenges with a fresh perspective.
• Adaptability: Being flexible in the face of change, adjusting to new situations, and learning quickly.
• Problem-solving: Analyzing situations, identifying solutions, and making informed decisions to overcome challenges.
• Time Management: Efficiently organizing and prioritizing tasks to meet deadlines and achieve goals.
• Critical Thinking: Evaluating information, considering multiple perspectives, and making reasoned judgments.
• Conflict Resolution: Addressing and resolving disagreements constructively, promoting positive working relationships.
• Emotional Intelligence: Recognizing and understanding emotions, both in oneself and others, to navigate social situations effectively.

Now, gaining soft skills can happen in various ways that might interest you:

- **Leadership Programs:** Participating in leadership programs allows you to develop skills like effective communication and accountability.
- **Sports:** Engaging in sports not only keeps you active but also teaches teamwork, communication, and adaptability.
- **Playing Games:** Playing games isn't just fun; it also promotes creativity, problem-solving, and teamwork.

- **Journaling:** Keeping a journal helps you reflect on yourself and become more self-aware, which is crucial for effective communication.
- **Being Social:** Simply hanging out with friends and engaging with others helps you develop interpersonal skills, empathy, and the ability to handle conflicts.

So, while it's important to focus on your hard skills, don't forget to nurture these soft skills too. They not only make your work environment more positive but also set you on a path for long-term success in your career.

It's clear how your values, interests, and passion all come together to shape what you might want to do in the future. Think of it like this: what you care about (your values) plays a big role in what you like to do (your interests) and what you really, really love (your passion). When you connect what you care about to what you enjoy, it helps you figure out what you're super passionate about.

And here's the cool part... When you're passionate about something, you naturally get better at it. It's like practicing a video game or a sport; the more you do it, the more skills you pick up. Now, we will show you a whole bunch of different jobs and careers out there. It's like opening a door to a room full of possibilities, where you can explore all kinds of cool stuff that matches up with what you're into and what you're good at.

Get ready for a journey of discovery!

WHAT CAN YOU DO?

> *Efforts and courage are not enough without purpose and direction.*
>
> — *JOHN F. KENNEDY*

"I'm going for that unicorn in the corner," Emily declares, excitement evident in her voice.

Alex, analyzing the machine, suggests, "I think the teddy bear right by the chute is a solid choice. What do you think, Lily?"

Lily, with a keen eye for detail, spots a fluffy kitten among the toys. "I've got my eyes on that adorable kitten over there," she says, pointing.

They each take turns, inserting coins and maneuvering the claw with precision. Laughter and friendly banter fill the air as they cheer each other on.

"Come on, Emily, you can do it!" Alex encourages.

The claw descends, gripping the unicorn firmly. Cheers erupt as Emily successfully snags her coveted prize.

Lily takes her turn next, and the claw carefully lifts the fluffy kitten, securing it in its grasp. "Yes! I got it!"

Amidst the playful competition, Alex makes his move for the teddy bear. "Fingers crossed," he mutters, guiding the claw to his chosen target.

The machine hums, and the teddy bear is lifted, completing the trio's successful conquest of the claw machine. Their laughter echoes through the arcade as they celebrate their newfound stuffed companions.

As they step away from the claw machine, Lily reflects on their successful endeavor, "You know, choosing the right stuffed animal in the game is a lot like picking a career path in real life."

Curious, Emily and Alex turn to Lily, intrigued by the comparison. Lily continues, "Just like we considered which prize to pick... we should do the same when deciding on our career paths. You know, based on our skills, interests, and values. It's about finding something that truly resonates with who we are."

Emily nods, "So, it's not just about what looks good or what others are doing, but what feels right for us?"

"Exactly," Lily responds. "Just like how we each had a strategy for the claw machine, we should have a plan for our careers based on what we enjoy and what aligns with our values."

Continuing their conversation, Emily, Alex, and Lily delve into the vast world of career possibilities. They discuss the various industries and positions that cater to different skills and interests they explored in the previous chapter.

Emily mentions, "It's fascinating how there are so many paths to choose from, each requiring a unique set of skills and passions."

Alex adds, "Yeah, it's not just about traditional jobs. There are careers in art, technology, healthcare, and more. It's like a buffet of opportunities out there."

Lily chimes in, "And just like we strategize for the claw machine, we can plan our approach to choosing a career. Understanding our values will guide us to something fulfilling."

As they share insights and discoveries, the friends find themselves excited about the prospect of exploring diverse careers that align with their individual strengths and passions. The wide range of possibilities unfolds before them, sparking curiosity and anticipation for the journeys they may embark on in the future.

Choosing a career can be overwhelming, much like when Emily, Alex, and Lily navigate the stuffed animals in a claw machine game. We will now explore the vast world of career options, acknowledging the challenge teens face in making decisions at a young age. We understand the struggle of selecting from countless jobs because we know how you feel in this complex decision-making process.

To alleviate concerns, rest assured that our insights will help you understand that choosing a career isn't a final decision. We encourage you to view it as a dynamic journey where adjusting goals and even changing careers is a natural part of the process. The key to starting your career pursuit is understanding yourself.

This next chapter further introduces tools for finding the right fit, with personality and aptitude tests emerging as introspective tools.

We will learn how individual traits can align with various professions. You will be able to rest assured that, despite the overwhelming number of career possibilities, taking steps towards self-awareness and exploration lays a solid foundation for pursuing any goal. The journey may seem vast, but with the right mindset and understanding, you can navigate the path to a fulfilling and meaningful career.

A WORLD OF OPTIONS

Choosing a career can feel like trying to figure out a giant maze, with so many paths and turns that it seems impossible to know which way to go. This is especially true for teens who are just starting to make big decisions about their future. Deakin University published an excellent article that emphasizes how the "options can seem endless and overwhelming. And many high school students worry about choosing the wrong career", which is why it's so important to have a proper mindset when doing so.

There are a ton of career choices out there, and it's totally normal for teens to feel stressed about picking the right one. It's like staring at a massive menu and not knowing what to order. The good news is that this book will provide tips regarding how to make this decision a bit easier, so you don't have to feel so lost in the sea of possibilities.

We get it - the sheer number of options is like navigating an intricate labyrinth, and it's easy to get lost in the complexity of making such a significant decision.

But here's the cool part – there's no way that you will be left hanging in this sea of uncertainty. Luckily, this book is like a friendly guide, ready to help you navigate the maze. Consider our insights like a flashlight, giving some direction on how to approach this massive decision. It's a reassuring hand on your shoulder, saying, "Hey, it's okay to feel overwhelmed, and we've got some tricks to make it a bit easier for you." So, even though choosing a career might feel like staring at a puzzle with a million pieces, there are ways to help you put it all together.

You see, picking a career path isn't like selecting a character in a video game... It's not final. Life's journey is more like a customizable game where you can unlock new levels and explore different realms. If you ever find yourself on a career path that doesn't quite spark the joy you expected, guess what? You're not stuck! You have the power-up to switch careers and find the path that aligns better with your passions and interests.

In the wise words of career explorer Utkarsh Amitabh, "Career transitions are like Shrek. They're complex and there is usually a lot more to them than we see on the surface, so you'll need to unpack the layers one at a time." Your career journey is dynamic, and filled with countless opportunities to explore.

Your career journey is like a dynamic video game with countless opportunities to explore. Don't stress too much if you're not sure which power-up to grab just yet. Feel free to change characters, try new quests, and level up as you go. Adjusting goals along the way is totally expected because, let's face it, life's twists and turns are what make the adventure so epic!

Remember, you're not stuck with your first choice, and there's no "Game Over' screen in your career journey. Embrace the adventure, stay curious, and trust that each move you make is a step closer to unlocking your unique, awesome path.

Embarking on the journey to pursue a career can feel like setting sail on uncharted waters. The first and crucial step in navigating this vast sea of possibilities is to understand yourself. This isn't just about listing your skills or jotting down your interests; it's about a deep, introspective dive into who you are, what you value, and where you envision yourself in the future.

Take a moment to sit with yourself, much like a seasoned sailor pondering the vastness of the ocean. Reflect on what you truly want from your career, whether it's financial stability, a harmonious work-life balance, personal fulfillment, or a blend of all these elements. Consider your values, strengths, interests, and even your preferred work style. Imagine your career as a ship, and you are the captain steering it towards uncharted territories.

This self-reflection process is akin to creating a treasure map of occupations that resonate with your inner compass. If you find joy in helping people and prefer a hands-on role, occupations like carer, disability worker, or counselor might align with your aspirations. Understanding your traits and preferences will make the vast array of career choices more navigable.

However, this journey doesn't have to be a solo expedition. If you find yourself lost in the sea of options, seek guidance from career counselors, coaches, or even friends and family members who can serve as your trusted navigators. They can ask you the right questions and help you chart a course that aligns with your aspirations.

In essence, understanding yourself is the North Star that will guide you through the often overwhelming process of choosing a career. Just as a sailor needs to know the winds and currents, knowing your values, strengths, and interests will make it easier to navigate the twists and turns of the professional landscape. So, set your sails, understand your compass, and may your career journey be as fulfilling as the horizon that stretches before you.

WHERE INTERESTS MEET SKILLS

In the vast landscape of career possibilities, it's essential to recognize that industries and specific jobs can be more than just avenues for earning a living—they can align seamlessly with your values and interests, creating a fulfilling and purposeful professional journey.

Consider industries as vast continents, each with its unique terrain and offerings. If you are passionate about making a positive impact on society, you might find fulfillment in the expansive landscape of community services. This sector, akin to a vibrant and diverse ecosystem, harbors roles like social workers, counselors, or community organizers, allowing you to directly contribute to the well-being of others.

Zooming in further, individual jobs within these industries can be seen as distinct landscapes within the broader continent. Just as a traveler might explore different cities within a country, you can explore various roles that align with your values and interests. If creativity fuels your passion, roles in graphic design, content creation, or artistic endeavors might be the bustling urban centers within the creative industry where you find your niche.

Crucially, understanding that industries and jobs can align with values and interests transforms the job search from a mere quest for employment into a deliberate expedition toward personal fulfillment. If you value innovation, the tech industry may be your futuristic haven, with roles in artificial intelligence, software development, or data science providing the thrill of discovery and advancement.

Imagine your values and interests as a compass guiding you through this vast career terrain. When you align your professional choices with what matters to you on a personal level, work becomes more than just a means to an end—it becomes a purposeful journey where each step is infused with meaning.

So, whether you find yourself in the lush greenery of environmental advocacy, the dynamic metropolis of business and entrepreneurship, or the serene landscapes of healthcare, know that the career world is rich with opportunities that resonate with your values and interests. The key is to navigate with intention, explore the terrains that speak to your soul, and build a career landscape that reflects the essence of who you are.

Specific jobs and how they can align with your interests and skills:	Industries and how they can align with values and interests:
• Architect (Arts and Design): If you have a passion for creativity, an eye for aesthetics, and love visualizing spaces, becoming an architect might be a perfect fit. Architects design buildings and spaces, bringing artistic vision to life while considering functionality and practicality. • Legal Secretary (Law and Record-keeping): For those intrigued by the legal world, a career as a legal secretary could be exciting. Your organizational skills and attention to detail will shine as you assist lawyers, maintain records, and ensure the smooth flow of legal processes. • Biochemist (Science and Problem-Solving): If you're fascinated by the intricacies of living organisms and enjoy solving scientific puzzles, a biochemist role might be ideal. Biochemists study the chemical processes within and related to living organisms, contributing to advancements in medicine, agriculture, and more.	• News Media (Truth and Content Creation): If you value truth, storytelling, and staying informed, the news media industry could be a perfect match. Working as a journalist or content creator allows you to contribute to the dissemination of accurate information, shaping public understanding and awareness. • Fundraising (Charity and Events): For individuals passionate about making a positive impact, fundraising offers an avenue to support causes close to your heart. Whether organizing events, managing campaigns, or building relationships with donors, you play a crucial role in raising funds for charitable initiatives. • Politics (Community Service and Legislation): Those driven by a sense of community service and a desire to shape policies can find fulfillment in the political arena. Whether as a lawmaker, policy analyst, or community organizer, you contribute to creating positive change and representing the interests of the public.

- Graphic Designer (Visual Arts and Technology): Combining artistic flair with technological know-how, a graphic designer creates visually appealing designs for various purposes. Whether it's crafting logos, designing websites, or working on marketing materials, your creativity and tech skills can shine in this role.
- Environmental Scientist (Nature and Research): Nature enthusiasts with a passion for preserving the environment can find fulfillment as environmental scientists. By conducting research and analysis, these professionals contribute to understanding and addressing environmental issues, promoting sustainable practices.
- Software Developer (Technology and Coding): If you're intrigued by the world of technology and enjoy coding, a career as a software developer awaits. You get to create software applications, solve complex problems, and contribute to the ever-evolving tech landscape.
- Psychologist (Human Behavior and Empathy): Those with a keen interest in understanding human behavior and offering support can thrive as psychologists. Whether in clinical settings, schools, or organizations, psychologists use their empathy and analytical skills to help individuals navigate challenges.
- Chef (Culinary Arts and Creativity): Culinary enthusiasts who love experimenting in the kitchen can pursue a career as a chef. Your creativity comes to life as you craft delicious and visually appealing dishes, delighting the taste buds of those who savor your creations.
- Education (Knowledge and Mentorship): If you value knowledge and enjoy helping others learn and grow, the education sector may be your calling. Whether as a teacher, academic advisor, or education administrator, you contribute to shaping the future by imparting knowledge and fostering personal development.
- Technology (Innovation and Problem-Solving): Individuals fascinated by innovation and solving complex problems may find their niche in the technology industry. Whether as a software developer, data scientist, or IT specialist, you contribute to advancements that shape the way we live and work.
- Healthcare (Compassion and Patient Care): Those with a deep sense of compassion and a desire to make a difference in people's lives may thrive in the healthcare sector. Whether as a nurse, doctor, or healthcare administrator, you contribute to the well-being of individuals and communities.
- Environmental Conservation (Sustainability and Nature): If preserving the environment aligns with your values, a career in environmental conservation allows you to contribute to sustainability efforts. Whether as a conservation scientist, environmental engineer, or wildlife biologist, you work towards protecting the planet.
- Entertainment Industry (Creativity and Performance): Creative individuals who enjoy entertaining others may find their passion in the entertainment industry. Whether as an actor, musician, or filmmaker, you have the opportunity to bring joy, inspiration, and emotional connections to audiences.

Remember, the key is to align your interests and skills with a career that brings you joy and fulfillment. Exploring various options within your areas of passion can open doors to exciting and rewarding professional journeys. Likewise, finding a career in an industry that aligns with your values and interests not only brings personal satisfaction but also contributes to a meaningful and fulfilling professional journey. Explore different sectors, discover your passions, and pursue a path that resonates with who you are.

 NASA needs workers who have a wide variety of knowledge and skills. NASA isn't just astronauts and scientists. NASA has engineers, mathematicians, accountants, writers, IT specialists, project managers, public relations managers, and more. The most important thing for preparing to find a job at NASA is that you study what you like and work hard to achieve your goals.

— NASA CAREERS FAQ

In the world of industries, it's important to understand the wide range of jobs available within each sector. Contrary to what many may think, creativity isn't limited to traditional artistic fields alone; it extends into areas like healthcare, technology, and finance. Similarly, objectivity, often thought to belong to specific sectors, can be found across various fields. Whether you're interested in the creative aspects of film production or the structured world of healthcare administration, there are diverse career options to explore. From roles in the performing arts to supporting services in healthcare, every industry offers a variety of jobs. This realization means that individuals can find careers that not only match their skills but also ignite their passions, creating a diverse and thriving professional landscape.

Examples of Different Industries and the Extensive Range of Jobs They Encompass	
Creative Industry: Film and Entertainment	Industry: Healthcare

Creative Industry: Film and Entertainment

Film Production:
- Director
- Producer
- Cinematographer
- Film Editor
- Production Designer
- Costume Designer
- Makeup Artist
- Sound Engineer
- Visual Effects Artist

Performing Arts:
- Actor/Actress
- Stage Manager
- Choreographer
- Set Designer
- Lighting Technician
- Costume Designer
- Makeup Artist
- Sound Technician

Music Industry:
- Musician/Composer
- Record Producer
- Sound Engineer
- Music Manager
- Booking Agent
- Music Journalist
- Concert Promoter
- Music Therapist

Media and Communications:
- Film Critic/Reviewer
- Entertainment Journalist
- Public Relations Specialist
- Social Media Manager
- Talent Agent
- Event Coordinator
- Marketing Specialist
- Animation and Visual Effects

Animator:
- 3D Modeler
- Storyboard Artist
- Texture Artist
- Rigging Artist
- Visual Effects Supervisor
- Lighting Artist
- Character Designer

Industry: Healthcare

Clinical Healthcare:
- Physician/Doctor
- Nurse
- Surgeon
- Medical Laboratory Scientist
- Radiologist
- Pharmacist
- Physical Therapist
- Occupational Therapist

Healthcare Administration:
- Hospital Administrator
- Healthcare Manager
- Health Informatics Specialist
- Medical Office Manager
- Healthcare Consultant
- Health Policy Analyst
- Medical Coder
- Health Services Manager

Research and Development:
- Medical Researcher
- Clinical Research Coordinator
- Biomedical Engineer
- Pharmacologist
- Geneticist
- Epidemiologist
- Research Analyst

Diagnostic Services:
- Medical Imaging Technologist
- Clinical Laboratory Technologist
- Pathologist
- Sonographer
- Phlebotomist
- Cardiovascular Technologist

Public Health:
- Epidemiologist
- Health Educator
- Environmental Health Specialist
- Public Health Analyst
- Community Health Worker
- Health Policy Advocate

Support Services:
- Medical Administrator
- Health Information Technician
- Medical Transcriptionist
- Patient Services Representative
- Medical Librarian
- Medical Interpreter

These examples showcase the incredible variety of professions found within every industry, driving home a crucial point: creativity isn't confined solely to traditional artistry but extends its reach into unexpected territories such as healthcare, technology, and finance. Similarly, the concept of objectivity, often linked to specific sectors, breaks down barriers and influences fields across the board. What unfolds from these instances is a diverse tapestry of career options, demonstrating that passion and proficiency can align in myriad ways. Whether one is drawn to the dynamic creativity of film production or the structured precision of healthcare administration, each industry offers a range of opportunities tailored to individual skills and interests. This realization expands the horizons of professional possibilities, illustrating that the professional landscape is diverse and abundant with opportunities for those with varied skills and passions.

Navigating the intersection of skills and interests can sometimes feel like a daunting task, as these two aspects may initially appear conflicting. However, the intricate dance between skills and interests often uncovers hidden synergies that lead to occupations perfectly tailored to an individual's unique blend of abilities and passions. By strategically combining specific industries and job roles, individuals can discover career paths where their skills complement their interests, fostering a sense of fulfillment and professional satisfaction. This harmonious convergence not only defies the notion of a stark dichotomy between skills and interests but also opens up a realm of opportunities where individuals can thrive by leveraging their distinctive qualities in tandem. In essence, finding the sweet spot between skills and interests involves exploring the vast landscape of occupations that harmoniously merge both elements, creating a fulfilling and rewarding professional journey.

TOOLS FOR FINDING THE RIGHT FIT

One amazing tool for self-discovery is a personality test. If you take a personality test or aptitude test, you will find out things about yourself that you didn't even know about. This could go a long way to selecting the right career. In his article, *How Personality Tests Might Help You Find a Job You'll Love*, Luke Smillie explains that these assessments aren't like traditional tests with right or wrong answers. Instead, they help describe your typical ways of behaving, feeling, and thinking... Basically, what makes you, well, you.

Imagine if a friend was recommending you for a job, they might describe you as hard-working, outgoing, or friendly. That's essentially describing your personality.

Simillie emphasizes that personality assessments, despite being called tests, don't have right or wrong answers. They use self-report questionnaires to gather descriptions of your traits, like how talkative, outgoing, or sociable you think you are. When it comes to job searching, these assessments are thought to predict how likely you'd enjoy and succeed in a certain job.

One interesting idea Similie brings up is "person-occupation fit," suggesting that people tend to thrive more in jobs that match their personalities. So, taking a personality test could help you figure out what kinds of jobs might suit your interests, traits, and characteristics. However, the article warns that just getting a personality profile without any context or guidance might not be super helpful. It compares it to a music teacher helping you understand your vocal range... knowing that is useful, but it's even more beneficial when you're taught how to choose songs that match your voice. Similarly, personality assessments can guide you toward careers that align with your unique qualities when paired with advice on choosing the right path.

The Myers-Briggs Type Indicator (MBTI) is like a handy guide that helps you figure out your personality type and, in turn, guides you through the maze of career choices. According to the Myers Briggs Foundation, it's all about helping you find a career that matches your strengths and feels satisfying. Myers Briggs points out that your personality type isn't just a label; it influences how you approach career planning, the kind of work environment you might enjoy, what motivates you, and the tasks that you find interesting and rewarding.

It's like having a compass for your career journey. Myers Briggs is clear that the MBTI isn't meant for hiring decisions but is a tool to give you insights into tasks and roles that align with who you are. Research even backs this up, showing that people are most satisfied when they work in areas that play to their strengths and talents.

The passage encourages a well-rounded approach, suggesting that when you're exploring careers, it's not just about your personality type. You should also consider your interests, values, and abilities. The two middle letters of your type (ST, SF, NF, or NT) are particularly crucial in making career choices, the article notes.

Myers Briggs's main point is that the MBTI is all about finding the right fit between who you are and what you do. It stresses that while certain personalities might be drawn to specific careers, there's room for everyone in any career. As Myers Briggs puts it, "Your type preferences should not limit your choice in the work you choose to do."

In a nutshell, the Myers-Briggs test is like your personal career coach, helping you understand yourself better and make informed choices about your professional journey. It's not just about ticking boxes; it's about connecting the dots between your personality,

CAREER GUIDANCE FOR TEENS MADE SIMPLE | 45

interests, and career satisfaction, giving you the tools to navigate your career path with a deeper self-awareness.

Personality Types and Potential Jobs

ISFJ (Defender)

- Characteristics: Patient, detail-oriented, reliable, supportive, enjoys helping and uplifting others.
- Jobs: Teacher, Counselor, Nurse, Social Worker, Librarian, Human Resources Specialist, Office Administrator.

ENTP (Debater)

- Characteristics: Innovative, adaptable, enjoys problem-solving, thrives in diverse and challenging environments.
- Jobs: Entrepreneur, Salesperson, Consultant, Marketing Manager, Lawyer, Journalist, Research Scientist.

ESTP (Entrepreneur)

- Characteristics: Action-oriented, confident decision-maker, enjoys risks and challenges, sociable and adaptable.
- Jobs: Sales Representative, Business Owner, Emergency Responder (Paramedic, Police Officer), Athlete, Coach, Actor, Marketing Specialist.

Career and personality tests can be useful tools for exploring potential career paths, but it's important to understand that they aren't foolproof or the only solution to finding the perfect job. While these assessments can provide insights into your personality traits and strengths, they shouldn't be the sole basis for making career decisions.

We're all complex individuals and our interests and skills can change as we grow. So, while these tests offer some guidance, they're not definitive answers. It's crucial to approach them with an open mind and see them as just one piece of the puzzle.

Think of these tests as a starting point for self-reflection. They prompt you to consider different aspects of yourself, like your preferred work environment or how you like to solve problems. This self-awareness helps understand how your personality fits into various career paths.

Popular Personality Tests to Take
Myers-Briggs Type Indicator (MBTI):   Link: https://www.myersbriggs.org/   The MBTI assesses personality preferences based on four dichotomies: Extraversion/Introversion, Sensing/Intuition, Thinking/Feeling, and Judging/Perceiving.   DISC Assessment: Link: https://personality-quizzes.com/disc-test/?gad_source=1&gclid=CjwKCAiAiP2tBhBXEiwACslfni4OrGBp2IRAfxioUb EV98fqx-xUeLcSagZfJ53dcju5DhJIPR04jxoCBIYQAvD_BwE   DISC categorizes individuals into four personality traits: Dominance, Influence, Steadiness, and Conscientiousness, aiding in understanding communication styles and work preferences.   Big Five Personality Traits: Link: https://www.truity.com/view/tests/big-five-personality   Assessing Openness, Conscientiousness, Extraversion, Agreeableness, and Neuroticism, the Big Five model provides insights into one's general personality characteristics.   Holland Code (RIASEC):   Link:https://mypersonality.net/quiz?afid=gdnmps&gad_source=1&gclid=CjwKC AiAiP2tBhBXEiwACslfnmb44XGZCiqHybm5WG8MXN0WNja-DKMa0rGaY4wgauK7FWSqZyHlbBoCBdwQAvD_BwE   Assessing six personality types – Realistic, Investigative, Artistic, Social, Enterprising, and Conventional – this test aligns personality with compatible career choices.

These assessments can also help you identify your values and skills, giving you a foundation for evaluating potential careers. Knowing what's important to you and where your strengths lie can guide your decisions about your professional future.

However, it's essential to combine the insights from these tests with other experiences. Consider doing internships, talking to professionals in fields you're interested in, or getting involved in hands-on projects. Real-world experiences provide a more realistic view of different professions and help you make informed decisions about your career.

It's crucial to recognize that the world is full of endless possibilities when it comes to careers, and it's completely normal to feel overwhelmed by the myriad choices available. However, feeling overwhelmed shouldn't deter you; instead, consider it an opportunity to explore and discover what truly resonates with you.

There are steps that you can begin to take to provide yourself with the best foundation for pursuing any goal. The Seeing Strategy, which will be explained next, is an incredible tool that you can use as a lifeline to shine light on your journey. As we dive deeper, don't be afraid to explore, embrace change, and trust that each step forward is a valuable part of your unique career journey.

SERVING YOURSELF- THE SEEING STRATEGY

"Alright, who's up first?"

Emily, Alex, and Lily gather around the Jenga tower, their laughter filling the room as they prepare for a round of the classic game.

"I'll kick it off," Alex volunteers, "Let's see if I've got a steady hand today."

Alex, with a focused yet playful expression, carefully selects a wooden block from the tower, his fingers moving with precision to maintain its delicate balance.

"Good luck, Alex! Don't let it tumble too soon," Lily warns.

"Piece of cake!" he calls out when he successfully pulls the piece.

The trio engages in a friendly competition, taking turns removing and stacking blocks. Tension builds as the tower becomes increasingly precarious, yet the atmosphere remains light-hearted.

"This is getting intense. I hope it survives my turn," Emily muses.

Emily's hand hovers over the tower, carefully choosing her move, while Alex and Lily exchange playful banter. The room is filled with the distinctive sound of wooden blocks being shifted and the occasional gasp as the tower teeters on the edge.

"This tower is defying the laws of physics," Alex comments.

"Seriously, we're like Jenga wizards!" Lily exclaims.

As the game progresses, the friends share smiles and supportive cheers, creating a lively and enjoyable moment.

After the final Jenga piece is carefully placed, the tower intact, Lily takes a moment to reflect on the game's outcome.

"You know, playing Jenga got me thinking," she says. "Just like how we built this tower, positive self-esteem and good self-care are the sturdy foundation for the building blocks of life."

Emily nods in agreement, and Alex chimes in.

"Totally, Lily," Alex says. "It's like creating a strong base for everything else we do."

They gather around, sitting comfortably, ready to delve into a discussion about the broader implications of Lily's insight.

"It's true," Emily admits. "When we understand ourselves better, through things like personality tests, we can choose paths that align with who we are and what we value."

"And those values," Alex goes on, " they're like the glue holding everything together. Without a strong sense of what matters to us, it's easy for things to fall apart."

Lily smiles and picks up a wooden piece for emphasis. "Exactly! Just like in Jenga, where each piece relies on the others to stay standing. Our careers, relationships, and personal growth all interconnect."

The group reflects on the varied career paths discussed earlier and how understanding oneself can guide those choices.

"And when we talked about how career tests aren't the be-all and end-all, it makes sense. They're tools, not strict roadmaps," Emily points out.

Alex smiles. "Right. They help us explore possibilities, but it's up to us to decide what fits and what doesn't. Like choosing the right Jenga piece."

"And let's not forget that endless possibilities can be overwhelming," Lily reminds us. "That's where positive self-esteem comes in... trusting ourselves to navigate the choices."

As they wrap up their discussion, the friends realize that self-awareness, values, and positive self-esteem are the cornerstones of building a fulfilling life. Just like their carefully constructed Jenga tower, a strong foundation ensures a sturdy and resilient structure for whatever challenges may come their way.

In the journey of life, just like Emily, Alex, and Lily, every teen is on a quest to discover who they are and where they want to go. This chapter is like a roadmap, guiding you through the crucial landmarks of self-esteem, self-compassion, and self-care. Buckle up because understanding these concepts will set the stage for an epic adventure into your future.

First up, let's talk about self-esteem, the superhero cape you wear every day. It's not about being the coolest or the most popular; it's about believing in your own superpowers. Whether you're facing a challenging Jenga tower or the maze of life decisions, having confidence in yourself is like having a secret weapon.

Then, there's self-compassion, your trusty sidekick. It's about being kind to yourself, especially when you mess up or face tough times. Remember, even superheroes stumble, but it's the way they rise that defines them. So, cut yourself some slack and embrace the power of self-compassion.

Lastly, self-care is your superhero headquarters. Taking care of your mental health is like maintaining the Batmobile... it keeps you running smoothly. From the right fuel (positive vibes) to regular check-ups (mental breaks), self-care ensures you're equipped to handle whatever challenges come your way.

As you dive into this chapter, picture it as your superhero training ground. You'll encounter techniques and strategies that will help you build the superpowers of confidence, kindness to yourself, and a well-nurtured mind. By the end of the journey, you'll understand why treating yourself with love and respect isn't just a bonus but a crucial element that impacts your abilities, decisions, and overall well-being.

So, gear up, superhero-in-the-making! The adventure to discover your inner strengths and conquer the challenges of the future starts right here. Get ready to unlock the secrets of self-esteem, self-compassion, and self-care, and embark on the thrilling quest of shaping your own destiny.

WHY YOU SHOULD LOVE YOURSELF

Loving yourself is key.

Seriously, it is.

This is especially true when it comes to embracing your uniqueness and diversity. Feeling self-conscious is totally normal, especially as you're figuring things out during your teenage years. But here's the deal: everyone is different, and that's what makes life interesting.

When you love yourself, quirks and all, you're saying, "I'm awesome just the way I am." It's about embracing your individuality and being confident in who you are.

Loving yourself boosts your self-esteem and helps you feel comfortable in your own skin. Plus, it makes you more accepting of others and celebrates the diversity that makes the world colorful.

So, remember: embrace your uniqueness, celebrate your diversity, and love yourself for being you.

You're one of a kind, and that's pretty cool.

Know Your Identity

Understanding why it's important to be yourself and develop your own identity is a big part of learning to love who you are. As the researchers Yuriy Gorodnichenko and Gerard Roland put it, "Countries having a more individualist culture have enjoyed higher long-run growth than countries with a more collectivist culture." Think about it like this: just as some countries with cultures that celebrate individuality do really well in terms of new ideas and growth, when you embrace your uniqueness, it sets you up for success, too.

Gorodnichenko and Roland assert, "When you're true to yourself, you get to know what makes you awesome, what you're good at, and what you love doing." This is just like how individualist cultures attach social status rewards to personal achievements, providing both monetary incentives for innovation and social status rewards.

It's kinda like how in places where people are encouraged to chase their dreams and be different, cool stuff happens. It's the same with you. When you're all about being yourself, you're more likely to feel happy and fulfilled.

Plus, when you're confident in who you are, you can handle whatever life throws your way. Just like how in those places where people are celebrated for their individuality, they're better at dealing with challenges and making things happen. You can, too.

So, embracing who you are and finding your own identity isn't just about feeling good about yourself... although that's a big part of it. It's also about being ready to take on the world and make your mark just by being you.

What is YOUR Identity?

Your identity, by definition, cannot be decided by anyone but you.
Use these examples as a guide to what resonates most with YOU.

1. Sports Enthusiast: Teens who excel in or are passionate about sports often identify strongly with their athletic abilities and achievements.
2. Music Lover: Teens who enjoy playing instruments, singing, or simply listening to music may find a significant part of their identity in their taste in music and musical talents.
3. Academic Achiever: Students who prioritize their studies and excel in school may see themselves primarily as scholars, valuing intelligence and academic success.
4. Artist/Creative: Teens who are skilled in visual arts, writing, or other creative pursuits often identify strongly with their artistic talents and may express themselves primarily through their creative endeavors.
5. Gamer: Teens who enjoy playing video games may identify strongly with gaming culture, spending a significant amount of time immersed in virtual worlds and connecting with others through online gaming communities.
6. Social Activist: Teens who are passionate about social justice issues may identify as activists, advocating for causes they believe in and working to create positive change in their communities and the world.
7. Bookworm: Teens who love reading and literature may identify strongly as bookworms, finding joy and solace in the pages of their favorite books and connecting with others who share their passion for reading.
8. Tech Geek: Teens who are fascinated by technology, computers, and gadgets may identify as tech geeks, embracing their love for all things tech-related and staying up-to-date on the latest innovations and trends.
9. Outdoor Adventurer: Teens who enjoy spending time outdoors, hiking, camping, or participating in outdoor sports may identify as outdoor adventurers, valuing nature and seeking out new outdoor experiences.

If what you are into is not listed, that's *perfect!*
The true version of YOU is different, unique, and special.

So, what calls to YOU?

- _____
- _____
- _____

Know Your Diversity

Diversity at work is super important because it helps bring out the best in everyone. You know how when you're in a group project at school and everyone has different ideas? Well, it's kinda like that but on a bigger scale. Having people from various backgrounds and with different perspectives can lead to some really cool ideas and solutions. As highlighted in the article, *How Diversity Makes Us Smarter*, Katherine Phillips presents research showing that diversity of expertise and backgrounds leads to better decision-making and problem-solving. When teams consist of individuals with different perspectives, they bring unique information and experiences to the table, which encourages the exploration of novel ideas and alternative solutions.

Think about it this way: if you're building something, you wouldn't just want a bunch of people who know the same stuff. You'd want engineers, designers, and all sorts of experts to make sure everything turns out awesome. It's the same with diversity in the workplace. Phillips explains that "diversity enhances creativity. It encourages the search for novel information and perspectives, leading to better decision-making and problem-solving." When you have a mix of people with different skills and experiences, you're more likely to come up with innovative ideas and make better decisions.

And get this! Studies have shown that companies with diverse leadership teams actually do better financially. Yeah, having a mix of all different kinds of folks at the top can lead to more value for the company and more cool stuff being created.

Plus, diversity makes research more exciting and impactful. When scientists from different backgrounds work together, they come up with better ideas and make more important discoveries. So, yeah, diversity isn't just a nice thing to have... it's a total game-changer in the workplace.

How Can Diversity Help YOU?

Diversity is special, sacred, and unique to only YOU.
Use these examples as a guide to see how it will help you in your career:

1. Creativity and Innovation: Having a diverse team means bringing together people with different perspectives, experiences, and ideas. This diversity sparks creativity and innovation, leading to the development of unique solutions and groundbreaking products or services.
2. Better Decision Making: When a team is composed of individuals from various backgrounds, they bring a range of viewpoints to the table. This diversity in perspectives helps in evaluating options more thoroughly, leading to more informed and effective decision-making processes.
3. Increased Problem-Solving Abilities: Diverse teams are often better equipped to tackle complex problems. With a variety of skills, knowledge, and approaches, team members can offer different insights and strategies for problem-solving, leading to more comprehensive and effective solutions.
4. Broader Market Understanding: A diverse workforce reflects the diversity of customers and clients. This enables companies to better understand and connect with their target audience, leading to improved customer satisfaction, loyalty, and ultimately, increased sales and profits.
5. Enhanced Employee Engagement and Satisfaction: Employees feel valued and respected when their organization embraces diversity. This fosters a positive work environment where everyone feels included and empowered to contribute their best, leading to higher levels of employee engagement, satisfaction, and retention.
6. Improved Reputation and Brand Image: Companies that prioritize diversity and inclusion are often viewed more favorably by customers, investors, and the general public. A commitment to diversity enhances a company's reputation as a socially responsible and progressive organization, which can attract top talent and loyal customers.
7. Global Expansion and Adaptability: In today's interconnected world, businesses operate in diverse markets with unique cultural norms and preferences. A diverse workforce is better equipped to navigate these differences and adapt to changing market conditions, enabling companies to expand globally and remain competitive.
8. Reduced Groupthink and Bias: Homogeneous teams may be prone to groupthink, where members conform to a consensus rather than critically evaluating alternatives. Diversity challenges this tendency by promoting healthy debate, constructive criticism, and a willingness to consider different viewpoints, leading to more thoughtful and balanced decisions.
9. Legal and Regulatory Compliance: Many countries have laws and regulations in place to promote diversity and prevent discrimination in the workplace. By fostering a diverse and inclusive environment, organizations can ensure compliance with legal requirements and mitigate the risk of costly lawsuits or reputational damage associated with discrimination.
10. Innovation and Research Excellence: In fields such as science, technology, and academia, diversity is essential for driving innovation and advancing knowledge. Collaborative research teams with diverse expertise and perspectives are more likely to make groundbreaking discoveries and contribute to the advancement of their respective fields.

Know How to Counter Self-Consciousness

"Feeling different" is totally normal during your teenage years. You're not alone if you sometimes feel self-conscious about how you look. In fact, most teens and even younger kids go through this.

Dr. Susan Woolford, who helped with this study, noticed that even younger kids are starting to feel bad about their appearance. It's not easy growing up with all these messages about how you should look.

But here's the thing: it's super important to accept yourself just the way you are. What's inside you matters way more than how you look on the outside. That's the real deal.

Parents can make a big difference here, too. Sometimes, they don't realize it, but when they complain about their own looks, it can make you feel worse about yourself. But if they focus on being healthy and remind you that everyone is beautiful in their own way, it can help.

Dr. Wendy Neal, a doctor who works with teens, says it's key for parents to listen when you talk about how you feel about your body. And they shouldn't brush off your concerns.

It's important to remember that there's no one-size-fits-all definition of beauty. Everyone is unique, and that's what makes you awesome. So, don't be too hard on yourself. Embrace who you are, and know that you're amazing just as you are.

Ways YOU Can Counter Self-Consciousness

1. Practice self-affirmations: Remind yourself of your strengths and what makes you unique.
2. Focus on what you love about yourself: Shift your focus from perceived flaws to positive attributes.
3. Surround yourself with supportive people: Spend time with friends and family who uplift and encourage you.
4. Engage in activities you enjoy: Pursue hobbies and interests that make you feel confident and fulfilled.
5. Practice self-care: Take care of your physical and mental well-being through exercise, healthy eating, and relaxation techniques.
6. Challenge negative thoughts: Challenge negative self-talk and replace it with more positive and realistic thoughts.
7. Set realistic goals: Set achievable goals for yourself and celebrate your successes along the way.
8. Avoid comparing yourself to others: Focus on your own journey and accomplishments rather than comparing yourself to others.
9. Seek professional help if needed: If self-consciousness is impacting your daily life, consider talking to a therapist or counselor for support and guidance.

So, the next time you find yourself feeling self-conscious or comparing yourself to others, remember this: you are enough just as you are. Embrace your individuality, celebrate your diversity, and love yourself for being uniquely you. After all, there's no one else in the world quite like you, and that's pretty amazing.

HOW TO CHANGE YOUR MIND

Having low self-esteem can make life feel like an uphill battle. It's like carrying around a heavy burden that weighs you down and holds you back from reaching your full potential. When you doubt yourself and your abilities, it's easy to fall into a cycle of negative thinking that can impact every aspect of your life.

On the other hand, having high self-esteem is like having a super-power. It gives you the confidence to tackle challenges head-on, believe in yourself, and pursue your dreams with determination.

When you have high self-esteem, you're more resilient in the face of setbacks, more willing to take risks, and more likely to achieve success in whatever you set out to do.

We believe that everyone deserves to feel confident and empowered in who they are. That's why we're committed to helping you build your self-esteem and unlock your full potential. Together, we'll explore the importance of self-compassion, self-acceptance, and self-love, and we'll provide you with the tools and resources you need to overcome self-doubt and embrace your unique strengths and talents. With the right mindset and the right support, you can build the self-esteem you need to thrive in every area of your life.

The Effects of Low Self-Esteem

Low self-esteem is a term used to describe a person's perception of themselves, particularly in terms of their value and worth. According to the University of Queensland's article on self-esteem and self-confidence, low self-esteem can be detrimental, leading individuals to feel negatively about themselves, their abilities, and their potential for success. It's characterized by a lack of appreciation or value for oneself, often influenced by negative experiences or internalized criticism. This negative self-perception can manifest in various ways, including self-doubt, feelings of inadequacy, and a tendency to focus on shortcomings rather than strengths.

The Effects of Low Self-Esteem
■ Shyness
■ Communication difficulties
■ Social anxiety
■ Lack of assertiveness
■ Avoidance of social situations
■ Fear of judgment or criticism
■ Negative self-talk
■ Perfectionism
■ Difficulty setting boundaries
■ Seeking validation from others
■ Difficulty making decisions
■ Feeling unworthy or inadequate
■ Fear of failure
■ Self-doubt
■ Difficulty accepting compliments or praise

The Effects of High Self-Esteem

High self-esteem is a positive perception and belief in one's own worth, value, and abilities. Individuals with high self-esteem tend to have confidence in themselves and their capabilities, viewing themselves in a positive light. They are able to acknowledge their strengths and weaknesses without allowing them to define their self-worth. Moreover, people with high self-esteem are often resilient in the face of challenges, as they possess a strong sense of self-assurance and inner security. They are more likely to pursue their goals with determination and optimism and they tend to maintain healthier relationships with themselves and others. In the article, *Is High Self-Esteem Beneficial? Revisiting a Classic Question*, Ulrich Orth explains that "having high (vs. low) self-esteem has wide-ranging positive consequences, including better social relationships, more success at school and work, better mental and physical health, and less antisocial behavior." Overall, high self-esteem fosters a sense of empowerment and well-being, contributing to a fulfilling and balanced life.

The Effects of High Self-Esteem

- More self-confidence

- Resistance to peer pressure

- Better mental health

- Greater resilience in facing challenges

- Improved relationships

- Increased motivation and drive

- Enhanced academic and professional performance

- Greater assertiveness

- Improved overall well-being and life satisfaction

How to Build Self-Esteem

Now that we understand the detrimental effects of low self-esteem, the next step is to explore how to overcome it. Thankfully, there are various strategies and techniques we can employ to boost our self-esteem and foster a more positive self-image. By utilizing resources like the provided list of methods to improve self-esteem, we can embark on a journey of self-discovery and personal growth. Through practices such as self-acceptance, reprogramming negative thought patterns, and setting achievable goals, we can gradually cultivate a stronger sense of self-worth and confidence. It's important to remember that building self-esteem is a process that takes time and effort, but with dedication and perseverance, positive change is indeed possible.

How to Build High Self-Esteem
■ Saying no
■ Making informed decisions
■ Positive self-talk/affirmations
■ Setting and achieving goals
■ Practicing self-care activities
■ Celebrating personal achievements, no matter how small
■ Surrounding yourself with supportive and positive people
■ Challenging negative self-talk and replacing it with positive affirmations
■ Learning new skills and hobbies
■ Engaging in regular physical activity and exercise
■ Accepting compliments gracefully
■ Helping others and contributing to your community
■ Taking pride in your accomplishments and strengths
■ Facing fears and stepping out of your comfort zone
■ Setting boundaries and advocating for yourself
■ Embracing failures as opportunities for growth
■ Seeking professional help or therapy if needed
■ Reflecting on past successes and moments of resilience

- Practicing gratitude and focusing on the positives in life

- Forgiving yourself for mistakes and past regrets

- Identifying and challenging negative beliefs about yourself

- Engaging in activities that bring you joy and fulfillment

- Recognizing your own worth and inherent value as a person

What Are Affirmations?

Affirmations are positive statements that you intentionally repeat to yourself as a way to challenge and overcome negative thoughts or beliefs. They are linked to better mental health because they can reshape your mindset, boost self-esteem, and promote a more optimistic outlook on life. Here are examples of some affirmations that you can try:

List of Affirmations
■ I can do anything I set my mind to.
■ I can learn anything I want to learn.
■ I have the power to make a difference in the world.
■ I know it's ok to make mistakes.
■ I have the power to control my thoughts and emotions.
■ I am a positive influence on those around me.
■ I am worthy of love and respect just as I am.
■ I embrace my uniqueness and celebrate my individuality.
■ I am capable of overcoming challenges and obstacles.
■ I believe in myself and my abilities to succeed.
■ I am confident in expressing my thoughts and opinions.
■ I am constantly growing and learning from my experiences.
■ I deserve to take care of myself and prioritize my well-being.
■ I am resilient and can bounce back from setbacks.
■ I am enough, exactly as I am, and I am deserving of happiness.
■ I trust myself to make choices that align with my values and goals.

Affirmations play a crucial role in nurturing better mental health. By focusing on strengths, affirmations provide positive reinforcement, fostering self-compassion and acceptance. They challenge negative thought patterns, instilling confidence and resilience while reducing stress and anxiety. Affirmations also enhance mood, promote self-reflection, and encourage self-awareness, all of which contribute to improved overall well-being. Through consistent practice, affirmations can reshape mindset, cultivate optimism, and ultimately build a strong foundation of self-esteem, enabling individuals to navigate life's challenges with greater confidence and resilience.

HOW TO LOVE YOURSELF BETTER

Affirmations are great.

Really, they are one of the most important things when it comes to building high self- esteem.

But, you know, it's not just about saying nice things to yourself; it's also about being kind to yourself, especially when things get tough. Think about it like this: you wouldn't be mean to your best friend if they were going through a hard time, right? So why do it to yourself? Self-compassion means treating yourself with the same kindness and understanding that you would show to a friend. It's about recognizing that you're not perfect, and that's okay. We all make mistakes, we all have bad days, and that's just part of being human.

Now, self-care is like giving yourself a little TLC. It's doing things that make you feel good, whether that's taking a bubble bath, going for a walk in nature, or just chilling out with some music. Self-care isn't selfish; it's necessary for your well-being. When you take care of yourself, you're better able to handle whatever life throws your way. Plus, it can help reduce stress, boost your mood, and improve your overall mental health.

Self-Care Tips for Teens

- Unplug Before Bed: Try to avoid screens (phones, tablets, computers) at least an hour before bedtime to help you unwind and get better sleep.

- Establish a Bedtime Routine: Creating a consistent bedtime routine signals to your body that it's time to wind down. Whether it's reading a book, taking a warm bath, or listening to calming music, find what relaxes you.

- Practice Mindfulness: Take a few minutes each day to practice mindfulness or meditation. This can help reduce stress and increase self-awareness.

- Limit Social Media Use: Set boundaries on your social media usage, such as using time limits or turning on "do not disturb" mode during certain times of the day to prevent distractions.

- Express Yourself Creatively: Engage in creative activities that you enjoy, whether it's drawing, painting, writing, or playing a musical instrument. Creative expression can be a great outlet for stress and emotions.

- Stay Active: Incorporate regular physical activity into your routine, such as going for a walk, practicing yoga, playing a sport, or dancing. Exercise not only benefits your physical health but also improves your mood and energy levels.

- Connect with Nature: Spend time outdoors and connect with nature. Whether you go for a hike, have a picnic in the park, or simply walk around your neighborhood, fresh air and sunshine can do wonders for your well-being.

- Practice Self-Compassion: Be kind to yourself and practice self-compassion. Treat yourself with the same kindness and understanding that you would show to a friend. Remember, it's okay to make mistakes and to take breaks when you need them.

- Stay Hydrated and Eat Well: Take care of your physical health by staying hydrated and eating nutritious foods. Fueling your body with the proper nutrients can help you feel better both mentally and physically.

- Get Enough Sleep: Prioritize getting enough sleep each night. Aim for 8-10 hours of quality sleep to support your overall health and well-being.

So, the next time you feel down or stressed out, remember to be kind to yourself. Give yourself a pep talk, practice some self-care, and remember that you're worthy of love and kindness, always.

INSIDE OUT

Mindfulness is defined as the awareness that arises when you intentionally pay attention in a kind, open, and discerning manner. It involves focusing on the present moment non-judgmentally. This practice encompasses two types of attention: focused attention, where concentration is directed toward a specific target, and open awareness, where you simply observe thoughts, feelings, or sensations as they arise and pass.

Mindfulness serves as an introspective tool by cultivating self-awareness and equipping you with essential life skills. It enhances equanimity, enabling you to allow sensory experiences to come and go without suppression or over-identification. Through concentration, mindfulness helps you focus on relevant tasks and goals, minimizing distractions and enhancing productivity. Moreover, mindfulness fosters sensory clarity, allowing you to accurately perceive and interpret your experiences in the present moment.

By practicing mindfulness, you develop a deeper understanding of yourself and your surroundings. This introspective awareness not only promotes personal growth but also aids in achieving outward goals. By cultivating mindfulness, you can harness your inner resources to navigate challenges, make informed decisions, and interact effectively with others. Overall, mindfulness serves as a powerful tool for introspection, facilitating both personal development and the pursuit of external objectives.

INTERACTIVE ELEMENT

A Guided Mindfulness Exercise

Here's a guided mindfulness exercise tailored to address feelings of anxiety, which is a relatable experience for many:

- Find a Comfortable Space: Start by finding a quiet and comfortable space where you can sit or lie down without distractions. Close your eyes if you feel comfortable doing so.
- Focus on Your Breath: Begin by taking a few deep breaths, inhaling slowly through your nose and exhaling through your mouth. Notice the sensation of the breath as it enters and leaves your body. Feel your chest rise and fall with each breath.
- Acknowledge Your Thoughts: As you continue to breathe, you may notice thoughts and worries entering your mind. Instead of trying to push them away, acknowledge them without judgment. Imagine each thought as a leaf floating down a stream, gently passing by.
- Ground Yourself in the Present: Shift your focus to your surroundings. Notice the feeling of your body against the chair or floor. Pay attention to any sounds you hear, whether it's the hum of appliances or the rustling of leaves outside. Engage your senses by noticing any smells or sensations in the environment.
- Practice Self-Compassion: If feelings of anxiety arise, remind yourself that it's okay to feel this way. Offer yourself words of kindness and reassurance, such as "It's normal to feel anxious sometimes, and I'm doing the best I can." Treat yourself with the same compassion you would offer a friend in a similar situation.
- Return to Your Breath: Whenever you feel your mind wandering or becoming overwhelmed, gently guide your attention back to your breath. Focus on the rhythm of your breathing, allowing it to anchor you in the present moment.
- Embrace Stillness: Take a few more moments to simply be still and present with yourself. Allow any tension or anxiety to melt away as you continue to breathe deeply.
- Conclude with Gratitude: Before ending the exercise, take a moment to express gratitude for this opportunity to practice mindfulness and self-care. Recognize the strength and resilience within yourself to navigate difficult emotions.
- Slowly Transition: When you're ready, gradually bring your awareness back to your surroundings. Wiggle your fingers and toes, stretch your body gently, and open your eyes if they are closed.

Remember that mindfulness is a skill that takes practice, so be patient with yourself as you explore this exercise. With regular practice, you can cultivate a greater sense of calm and resilience in the face of anxiety.

Mindfulness serves as a sturdy foundation upon which we can build our mental and emotional well-being. By cultivating awareness, self-compassion, and resilience, we lay the groundwork for navigating life's challenges with greater ease and clarity. Just as a strong foundation supports the structure above it, mindfulness provides stability and grounding in the face of uncertainty and stress. With this foundation in place, we can begin to build upon it, exploring additional practices and strategies to further enhance our well-being. Whether it's through guided mindfulness exercises, self-care practices, or cultivating positive affirmations, we have the tools we need to continue our journey toward greater self-awareness and inner peace. By investing in our mindfulness practice, we empower ourselves to lead more fulfilling and balanced lives.

EXCELLING ACADEMICALLY

"The more that you read, the more things you will know. The more that you learn, the more places you'll go."
—Dr. Seuss

"Wow, this place brings back so many memories!"

Emily, Alex, and Lily stroll down the street, their footsteps echoing against the pavement as they pass by their old elementary school. Memories flood back as they reminisce about their time there.

"I know, right?" Emily asks. "I mean, do you remember when we had to do that science project in Mrs. Johnson's class?"

Alex nods, a reminiscent gleam in his eyes. "Yeah, that volcano experiment was a blast. Literally."

Lily chuckles. "I still can't believe we managed to make it erupt without setting off the fire alarm."

"It was all thanks to your baking soda skills, Lily," Alex teases, nudging her playfully.

As they chat animatedly, their laughter fills the air, mingling with the sounds of passing cars and chirping birds. Despite the passage of time, their bond remains strong, and the shared experience of working together on that project serves as a reminder of the enduring friendships forged in childhood.

Emily reflects, "You know, that science project taught us more than just about chemical reactions."

Alex nods in agreement. "Yeah, it taught us about teamwork. Remember how we had to brainstorm ideas together and divide up the tasks?"

Lily smiles warmly. "And even when things didn't go as planned, we stuck together and figured it out."

"It was like our own little laboratory of teamwork," Emily adds, a sense of pride evident in her voice.

As they reminisce about their elementary school project, Lily quotes, "'The more that you read, the more things you will know. The more that you learn, the more places you'll go.'"

Alex tilts his head toward Lily. "Is that a Dr. Suess quote?"

"Yes, it is!" She reflects on how their lesson on teamwork has transcended their school days, remaining relevant throughout their lives. "You know," Lily begins, "that Dr. Seuss quote really captures what we experienced back then. Learning to work together opened up so many opportunities for us, just like reading and learning do. It's amazing how those early lessons stick with us, guiding us through life's challenges and adventures."

Emily and Alex nod in agreement, their shared memories serving as a testament to the enduring power of collaboration and the valuable lessons they continue to carry forward into their adult lives.

* * *

Just as Emily, Alex, and Lily carried on the lessons learned from school into their lives, so too will you. This chapter delves into the significance of schooling, offering insights on how to maximize its benefits and navigate its limitations. While schooling equips us with academic knowledge, its true value lies in the development of skills that transcend the classroom and seamlessly transition into the professional realm. From critical thinking and problem-solving to collaboration and adaptability, these skills form the bedrock of success in any career path, regardless of academic interests. By understanding the transferability of these skills, you can harness the full potential of your educational journey and confidently navigate the challenges and opportunities that lie ahead in the professional world.

* * *

IT'S NOT JUST THE SUBJECTS

Going to school isn't just about learning math or history; it's also about learning how to handle stuff in your life, like getting things done on time, staying organized, and being responsible. You might not realize it, but all the homework, tests, and projects you deal with at school are actually helping you build these skills for later on, like when you have a job. Think about it: every time you finish a project or study for a test, you're practicing how to manage your time and stay on top of things. And when you work with other kids on a group project or play on a sports team, you're learning how to work together and get along with different people. Plus, school is a safe place to mess up and learn from your mistakes. So even though it might not always feel like it, everything you do at school is helping you get ready for whatever comes next.

SELF-DISCIPLINE

Self-Discipline
(noun)
The ability to make yourself do things you know you should do even when you do not want to.

Self-discipline is all about being able to control yourself and stick to your goals, even when it's tough. It means making choices that are good for you in the long run, even if they're not always fun at the moment. Like, instead of watching TV or playing video games all night, you might choose to study or finish your homework first because you know it'll help you in the future.

After high school, when you're out on your own, self-discipline becomes super important. You're responsible for yourself, your choices, and your future. Whether it's managing your time, sticking to a budget, or making healthy choices, having self-discipline can help you stay on track and reach your goals, even when there's nobody telling you what to do. It's like being your own boss and making sure you're doing what's best for you.

Self Discipline Techniques

- Removing temptations:
  - Example: Putting your phone on silent or using apps to block distracting websites while studying helps maintain focus and productivity.
- Setting up a dedicated study area:
  - Example: Designating a quiet corner of your room or using a specific table at the library for studying creates a conducive environment for concentration and learning.
- Being aware of your actions:
  - Example: Practicing mindfulness techniques, such as deep breathing or meditation, helps manage stress, improve concentration, and enhance overall well-being.
- Developing a routine:
  - Example: Establishing a daily schedule that includes regular study sessions, exercise, meals, and leisure activities promotes productivity, time management, and work-life balance.
- Setting SMART goals **(More information on this later)**:
  - Example: Breaking down large tasks into smaller, manageable goals with **S**pecific, **M**easurable, **A**chievable, **R**elevant, and **T**ime-bound criteria helps track progress and maintain motivation.
- Prioritizing tasks:
  - Example: Using techniques like the Eisenhower Matrix to categorize tasks based on urgency and importance allows for better time allocation and effective decision-making. The Eisenhower Matrix is a powerful tool for managing tasks and making decisions. It helps individuals prioritize by categorizing tasks into four quadrants based on their urgency and importance. Tasks deemed urgent and important require immediate attention to prevent negative consequences or achieve critical objectives.
- Limiting multitasking:
  - Example: Focusing on one task at a time rather than attempting to juggle multiple tasks simultaneously reduces stress, improves concentration, and enhances productivity.
- Practicing self-care:
  - Example: Incorporating activities such as exercise, adequate sleep, healthy eating, and relaxation techniques into your routine promotes physical and mental well-being, leading to increased productivity and resilience.

By implementing these self-disciplinary techniques, you can cultivate habits that optimize productivity, foster personal growth, and support overall well-being as you transition from high school to other endeavors in life.

TIME MANAGEMENT

Time management is crucial in both higher education and the workplace, as highlighted by the article written by The Indeed Editorial Team, which states, "Many employers prioritize time management skills when recruiting employees." In higher education, effective time management allows students to meet deadlines for assignments, projects, and exams. Similarly, in the workplace, time management skills are essential for meeting project deadlines, completing tasks efficiently, and maximizing productivity. The Indeed Editorial Team emphasizes this by stating, "Time management is a vital skill for any employee because it determines your ability to meet deadlines and operate productively."

In higher education, good time management enables students to balance their academic workload with extracurricular activities, part-time jobs, and personal responsibilities. This is crucial for academic success and overall well-being. As the article suggests, "By allocating your tasks strategically, you can act based on your strengths and be more productive." Similarly, in the workplace, effective time management allows employees to prioritize tasks, avoid procrastination, and achieve work-life balance. This is emphasized by the article, which states, "Proper time management allows you to focus on a task at a time."

Overall, whether in higher education or the workplace, mastering time management skills is essential for success. By effectively managing your time, you can enhance your productivity, reduce stress, and achieve your academic and career goals.

Time Management Techniques
• Use schedules, planners, and calendars to organize your tasks and deadlines.
• Set reminders for important deadlines and tasks to stay on track.
• Prioritize your tasks based on urgency and importance.
• Estimate time frames for each task to allocate your time effectively.
• Break down large tasks into smaller, more manageable steps.
• Set specific goals and deadlines for each task to maintain focus and motivation.
• Avoid multitasking and focus on one task at a time to increase efficiency.
• Allocate time for breaks and relaxation to prevent burnout and maintain productivity.
• Learn to say no to tasks or commitments that are not essential or can be delegated to others.
• Review and adjust your schedule regularly to accommodate any changes or unexpected events.

Implementing these time management tips can help you effectively manage your time, increase productivity, and reduce stress in both academic and professional settings.

GOAL SETTING

Setting goals is like giving yourself a roadmap to success. It's not just about picking random targets; it's about figuring out what you want to achieve and creating a plan to get there. When you set goals, you give yourself something to strive for, which can boost your performance and keep you motivated along the way.

Think of it like this: imagine you're playing a video game without any objectives. Sure, you can wander around aimlessly, but it's much more satisfying when you have specific tasks to complete and levels to conquer. Goals work the same way in real life. When you have a clear goal in mind, whether it's acing a test, getting into your dream college, or landing your first job, it gives you something to focus on and work towards.

Setting goals also helps you measure your progress. Instead of feeling like you're just spinning your wheels, you can track your accomplishments and see how far you've come. This can be incredibly motivating because it shows you that your hard work is paying off.

Plus, achieving your goals feels amazing. Whether crossing off items on your to-do list or hitting a major milestone, reaching your goals gives you a sense of accomplishment and boosts your confidence. It's like leveling up in a game – each goal you achieve brings you one step closer to success.

So, whether you're aiming to improve your grades, make the varsity team, or land your dream job, setting goals is key to staying motivated and performing at your best. With clear objectives in mind, you'll have the focus and determination to overcome obstacles and make your dreams a reality.

SMART Goals
SMART goals are a framework for setting objectives that are clear, achievable, and effective. Each letter in "SMART" stands for a different criterion that helps ensure your goals are well-defined and actionable:

Criterion	Example
Specific: Your goal should be clearly defined and specific. Instead of saying, "I want to get better at math," a specific goal would be, "I want to improve my algebra skills by mastering factoring and solving equations."	"I want a better grade in my English class."
Measurable: Your goal should include clear criteria for measuring progress and success. This allows you to track your advancement and stay motivated. For example, you could measure progress by tracking the number of practice problems you complete each week or by monitoring your test scores.	"I will aim to raise my grade from a B- to an A- by the end of the semester."
Attainable: Your goal should be realistic and achievable. While it's great to aim high, setting goals that are too far out of reach can lead to frustration and disappointment. Make sure your goal is challenging but still within your capabilities and resources.	"I will achieve this by completing all homework assignments on time, studying for quizzes and tests regularly, and seeking help from my teacher or classmates when needed."
Relevant: Your goal should be meaningful and relevant to your overall objectives and aspirations. It should align with your values, interests, and long-term plans. Ask yourself why this goal matters to you and how it fits into your larger vision for your life.	"Improving my English grade is important to me because it will help boost my overall GPA and increase my chances of getting into the college of my choice."
Time-bound: Your goal should have a specific timeframe for completion. Setting a deadline creates a sense of urgency and helps you stay focused and motivated. Whether it's a week, a month, or a year, having a deadline gives you a clear target to work towards.	"I will accomplish this goal within the next three months, by the end of the current semester."

By following the SMART criteria, you can ensure that your goals are well-defined, achievable, and meaningful, setting yourself up for success and maximizing your chances of reaching your objectives.

SMART Goals Fill-In-The-Blank Template	
Use this fill-in-the-blank template to create your own SMART goal.	
Goal: _____	
S	
M	
A	
R	
T	

Learning time management, goal-setting, and other essential life skills while in a stable environment like high school is crucial to avoid feeling overwhelmed or underprepared for life after graduation. High school provides a supportive setting where students can experiment with new skills and interests without the pressure of the real world. It's the perfect time to try new things, explore different interests, and develop important skills that will benefit you in the future. As we transition into the next chapter, let's delve into how high school can be a place for self-discovery and growth.

YOUR TIME TO INSPIRE!

"The ones who are crazy enough to think they can change the world are the ones that do."

— *STEVE JOBS*

"Just think," Emily says, leaning back against the cafeteria wall and looking around the room. "In another ten years, everyone in this cafeteria will have a job. They'll know a bunch of people they've never met yet, and we'll probably never hear of them again."

Alex tears a piece off his sandwich and looks at her. "I can't decide whether that's depressing or exciting."

"It's exciting," Lily says firmly, spearing a piece of mango with her fork. "There are doctors, lawyers, writers, artists, engineers... all kinds of people in this room. And they haven't a clue who they're going to be yet. That's exciting."

"Yeah, but how are they going to find out?" Emily asks. "I think it's scary. Right now, they have no idea how they're going to get to where they're going to be – and half of them are doing their best to never think about the future right now."

Just like the kids in the cafeteria, your school is filled with people with bright and exciting futures in front of them – and just like those kids, many of them have no idea how they're going to get to it. You're already one step ahead of them. By reading this book, you're readying yourself to shape the course of your future... and this is your chance to help them do the same thing.

Just as Emily, Lily, and Alex are supporting each other's journeys through their discussions, you can help other teenagers direct their future – and that's as easy as taking a few minutes to write a short review.

By leaving a review of this book on Amazon, you'll help other teenagers who are searching for advice on how they can make sure they get the job of their dreams to find the guidance they're looking for.

You can bet your bottom dollar that there are other kids like you looking for this information online, and your review will show them where they can find it – all within less than five minutes of your time.

Thank you so much for your support. It might be hard to see how something so small can make such a big difference, but trust that it does.

Scan the QR code to leave your review!

amazon.com/review/create-review?&asin=B0D1WT5BX5

EXPLORING INTERESTS

> *The master has failed more times than the beginner has even tried.*
>
> — *STEPHEN MCCRANIE*

As the afternoon sun starts to dip, Emily, Alex, and Lily gather at their usual spot after their extracurricular activities.

"Man, that painting session was intense," Emily exclaims, carefully stowing away her brushes and canvases.

"I bet! But nothing compares to the rush of scoring a touchdown," Alex replies, still catching his breath from football practice.

Lily nods in agreement as she finishes packing her violin. "I had the most amazing rehearsal with the orchestra today. It's incredible how music brings us together."

The three friends share stories about their respective activities, each filled with passion and enthusiasm. As they chat, they can't help but feel grateful for the chance to explore their interests in such a supportive environment.

"Hey, you know what's cool about trying all these different hobbies?" Emily asks, a thoughtful expression on her face.

"What?" Alex and Lily chime in unison, curious.

"Well, besides having fun, it's like we're testing out different career paths without any pressure," Emily explains. "I mean, who knows? Maybe one of us will discover a hidden talent or a passion we never knew we had!"

"Totally!" Alex agrees. "And by reaching out for support and advice from people in these fields, we can get a better idea of what we might want to do in the future."

Lily nods enthusiastically. "Yeah, and even if we don't end up pursuing a career related to our hobbies, the skills we learn along the way are still super valuable."

The three friends smile, feeling grateful for the opportunities to explore and the supportive environment that encourages them to do so.

Sometimes, the answers to those big questions are right in front of us, hiding in plain sight.

Think about it.

What do you love doing in your free time? Maybe you're always doodling in your notebooks, or you spend hours perfecting your skateboard tricks at the park. Or maybe you're that person who's always baking up a storm in the kitchen or tinkering with gadgets to see how they work.

Believe it or not, those hobbies and extracurriculars could hold the key to your future careers. Yeah, seriously! Imagine turning your love for art into a career as a graphic designer or your passion for skating into a job as a sports coach. You could even become pastry chefs or engineers who invent the next big thing!

The point is, you don't have to have it all figured out right now. Sometimes, the best way to find your path is to look at what makes you happy and figure out how to turn that into a future you'll love. So, don't stress if you're not sure what career to pick just yet. Your hobbies and interests might just lead you right where you're meant to be.

FIND WHAT YOU LOVE

When we stick to what we know and never venture out of our comfort zone, we miss out on so much. We stay in our little bubble, never experiencing all the cool stuff that's out there waiting for us. But when we push ourselves to try new things, that's when the magic happens.

First off, trying new things helps us grow as people. We learn new skills, discover hidden talents, and develop strengths we never knew we had. It's like unlocking a whole new level of awesomeness within ourselves.

Plus, breaking out of our comfort zone builds confidence like nothing else. Yeah, it can be scary at first, but each time we try something new and succeed, we prove to ourselves that we're capable of more than we ever thought possible. And that confidence? It's like a superpower we can carry with us wherever we go.

But here's the best part: trying new things opens doors we never even knew existed. We meet new people, explore new places, and stumble upon opportunities we never could have imagined. Who knows? That random hobby or activity we decide to try on a whim could end up shaping our future in ways we never expected.

So, next time you're feeling stuck in a rut, challenge yourself to break out of your comfort zone and try something new. Whether it's joining a club, picking up a new hobby, or simply saying yes to that invitation you would normally decline, embrace the unknown and see where it takes you.

Trust me, it's worth it.

Tips for Selecting and Beginning New Hobbies or Activities.

- **Explore Your Interests:** Take some time to think about what genuinely interests you. Consider activities you've always wanted to try or topics that pique your curiosity.
- **Research:** Once you have a few ideas in mind, research them further. Look up classes, clubs, or local groups related to your interests. Check out online forums or social media groups for advice and recommendations.
- **Start Small:** Don't overwhelm yourself by diving into something too complex or time-consuming right away. Begin with simple, beginner-friendly activities or projects to ease yourself into the hobby.
- **Set Goals:** Determine what you hope to achieve or learn from your new hobby. Setting specific goals can help you stay focused and motivated as you progress.
- **Consider Cost and Accessibility:** Take into account the cost of supplies or equipment needed for your chosen hobby, as well as its accessibility in your area. Choose something that fits your budget and is easily accessible.
- **Take Advantage of Resources:** Utilize resources such as library books, online tutorials, or instructional videos to learn more about your chosen hobby before diving in.
- **Attend Workshops or Classes:** Consider signing up for introductory workshops or classes to get hands-on experience and guidance from experts in the field.

- **Find a Buddy:** Having a friend or family member join you in your new hobby can make the experience more enjoyable and provide accountability.
- **Be Patient:** Remember that learning something new takes time and practice. Don't get discouraged if you don't master it right away. Stay patient and enjoy the journey of learning and improvement.
- **Have Fun:** Above all, choose a hobby that brings you joy and fulfillment. Don't be afraid to experiment and explore different activities until you find the perfect fit for you.

Examples of Different Hobbies and How to Easily Practice Them

- **Drawing by following YouTube tutorials**
  - https://www.youtube.com/@SchaeferArt
  - https://www.youtube.com/@ALPHONSODUNN
  - https://www.youtube.com/@LethalChris1
- **Graphic design by using free apps**
  - Canva - https://www.canva.com/en_au/
  - Gimp - https://www.gimp.org/
  - Design Wizard - https://designwizard.com/
- **Coding with online courses**
  - Codecademy - https://www.codecademy.com/
  - Khan Academy - https://www.khanacademy.org/
  - Coursera - https://www.coursera.org/
- **Photography**
  - Start by using your smartphone camera to capture interesting scenes or objects around you.
  - Experiment with different angles, lighting, and composition techniques.
  - Join online photography communities or take a beginner's photography class to improve your skills further.

- **Cooking or Baking**
  - Start by trying out simple recipes for your favorite dishes or desserts.
  - Experiment with different ingredients, flavors, and cooking techniques.
  - Follow cooking blogs, watch instructional cooking videos, or take a beginner's cooking class to expand your culinary skills.
- **Gardening**
  - Begin by planting easy-to-grow herbs, flowers, or vegetables in pots or small garden beds.
  - Learn about basic gardening techniques such as watering, pruning, and fertilizing.
  - Join a local gardening club or attend gardening workshops to gain knowledge and connect with other enthusiasts.
- **Playing a Musical Instrument**
  - Choose an instrument that interests you and start practicing with beginner tutorials or online lessons.
  - Dedicate regular time to practice scales, chords, and simple songs.
  - Consider joining a community band or orchestra for additional guidance and performance opportunities.
- **Writing or Journaling**
  - Set aside time each day to write creatively or journal about your thoughts and experiences.
  - Experiment with different writing styles, genres, or prompts to stimulate your creativity.
  - Join writing workshops or online writing groups to receive feedback and support from fellow writers.
- **Yoga or Meditation**
  - Start by following beginner-friendly yoga or meditation videos online.
  - Practice simple breathing exercises, stretches, or mindfulness techniques to improve relaxation and focus.
  - Join a local yoga studio or meditation class to deepen your practice and connect with others.

- **DIY Crafts**
  - Explore different craft projects such as knitting, crocheting, sewing, or woodworking.
  - Start with easy-to-follow tutorials or beginner kits available online or at craft stores.
  - Join crafting communities or attend craft fairs to learn new techniques and share your creations with others.
- **Hiking or Nature Walks**
  - Discover local trails or nature parks to explore on foot.
  - Start with shorter, easier hikes and gradually increase the difficulty as you build endurance.
  - Bring along a field guide to identify plants, animals, and birds you encounter along the way.
- **Volunteering**
  - Get involved in community service projects or volunteer opportunities that align with your interests or values.
  - Research local organizations or charities in need of volunteers and reach out to offer your time and support.
  - Volunteering can provide valuable experience, meaningful connections, and a sense of purpose.

Stick To It

Sticking to hobbies can be challenging, but there are several strategies that can help you stay committed. First, it's essential to set realistic goals for yourself. Break down your hobby into smaller, achievable milestones, and celebrate your progress along the way. Creating a schedule and dedicating specific time each week to your hobby can also help you stay on track. Additionally, finding a buddy who shares your interests can provide motivation and support. Don't be afraid to mix things up and explore different aspects of your hobby to keep it interesting. It's essential to stay positive and focus on the enjoyment your hobby brings rather than getting discouraged by setbacks. Remember to be patient with yourself and acknowledge that mastery takes time and practice. Finally, take time to reflect on your progress and celebrate your achievements. By following these tips and staying dedicated, you can turn your hobby into a rewarding and long-lasting passion.

More Than Fun

Extracurricular activities are super important for teens because they offer a chance to explore new interests, make friends, and develop valuable skills outside of the classroom. Whether it's joining a sports team, participating in a club, or volunteering in the community, these activities provide opportunities for personal growth and development. They help us discover our passions, build confidence, and learn important life skills like teamwork, leadership, and time management. Plus, extracurriculars look great on college applications and can even lead to future career opportunities. Overall, getting involved in extracurricular activities is a fantastic way to make the most out of your high school experience and prepare for the future.

Extracurricular activities offer a dynamic platform for developing a wide range of skills, both hard and soft. Take learning an instrument, for instance. Beyond the joy of making music, it also sharpens decision-making and executive function skills. Whether it's choosing the next note or managing intricate rhythms, playing an instrument requires focus and quick thinking, which translates to better decision-making in other areas of life. Moreover, the perseverance needed to master an instrument teaches resilience— a vital skill in navigating life's challenges.

Similarly, sports provide more than just physical benefits. Engaging in athletics helps channel negative emotions into positive energy through exercise. The discipline and dedication required in sports build resilience, teaching participants how to bounce back from setbacks and push through adversity. Team sports also foster collaboration and communication skills which are crucial for success in any aspect of life.

Artistic pursuits, such as photography and drawing, encourage self-expression and creativity. They offer a means of communication beyond words, allowing individuals to convey their thoughts, feelings, and perspectives visually. Moreover, engaging in these activities hones tangible skills like attention to detail, spatial awareness, and hand-eye coordination—all of which have real-world applications in various fields.

In essence, extracurricular activities serve as fertile ground for cultivating a diverse skill set, encompassing both hard technical abilities and soft interpersonal skills. They provide invaluable opportunities for personal growth, enabling individuals to become more well-rounded and adaptable in an ever-changing world.

ASKING AROUND

You don't need to feel limited to choosing a career solely based on your extracurricular experiences. While these activities can provide valuable insights and skills, they're just one piece of the puzzle. Many successful professionals have ventured into careers that may seem unrelated to their hobbies or interests.

Instead of feeling pressured to make a definitive decision based solely on your extracurriculars, consider reaching out to people for advice and guidance. This could include speaking with mentors, teachers, family members, or professionals in fields of interest. These individuals can offer valuable perspectives, share their own career journeys, and provide insights into various industries.

By seeking advice from others, you can gain a broader understanding of the opportunities available to you and how your skills and interests may align with different career paths. This approach allows for exploration and discovery, empowering you to make informed decisions about your future without feeling constrained by your past experiences alone.

Who Can You Ask?

Professionals Working in the Occupation You Are Interested in

• **Tips on talking to someone about career advice:**
  ◦ Be Clear and Concise: Clearly explain your purpose for reaching out and what you hope to gain from the conversation.
  ◦ Be Respectful of Their Time: Acknowledge that their time is valuable and request a brief meeting or conversation.
  ◦ Prepare Thoughtful Questions: Come prepared with a list of questions about their career path, industry insights, and any specific concerns or interests you have.
  ◦ Express Gratitude: Thank them for their time and insights, regardless of the outcome of the conversation.
  ◦ Follow Up: If appropriate, follow up with a thank-you email expressing your appreciation for their advice and any next steps you plan to take.

- **Tips on how to contact someone to ask for career advice :**
  - LinkedIn: Use LinkedIn to search for professionals who are working in occupations you're interested in. Send them a personalized connection request explaining your interest in their field and politely ask if they would be open to a brief informational interview.
  - Networking Events: Attend networking events, career fairs, or industry conferences where professionals from various fields gather. Introduce yourself, express your interest, and ask if they would be willing to chat further about their career experiences.
  - Alumni Networks: Reach out to alumni from your school or university who are working in your desired field. Many alumni are happy to help fellow graduates and may provide valuable insights and advice.
  - Professional Organizations: Join professional organizations related to your field of interest. Attend their events, workshops, or webinars, and use these opportunities to connect with professionals and seek advice.
  - Cold Emails: If you don't have a direct connection, consider sending a polite and well-crafted cold email to professionals in your desired field. Introduce yourself briefly, explain your interest, and request a short informational interview or coffee chat.
  - Social Media: Utilize platforms like Twitter, Instagram, or Facebook to connect with professionals in your field. Engage with their content, ask thoughtful questions, and express your interest in learning more about their career path.
  - Professional Mentoring Programs: Explore mentoring programs offered by universities, community organizations, or professional associations. These programs pair students or aspiring professionals with experienced mentors who can provide guidance and advice.

Career Counselors

Career advisors play a crucial role in guiding individuals through the process of exploring career options, setting career goals, and making informed decisions about their professional paths. These professionals offer personalized support and resources to help individuals identify their strengths, interests, and value and align them with suitable career opportunities. They provide valuable insights into various industries, job trends, and educational pathways, helping individuals navigate the complexities of the job market.

Career advisors can be found in various institutions and organizations, including:

- Schools and Universities: Many educational institutions offer career counseling services to their students and alumni. These services may include individual counseling sessions, workshops, career fairs, and resources such as career assessments and job search tools.
- Career Centers: Stand-alone career centers or career development offices within educational institutions often provide comprehensive career counseling services. They may offer assistance with resume writing, interview preparation, internship placement, and networking opportunities.
- Government Agencies: Government-run employment centers or career services agencies often provide free or low-cost career counseling and job search assistance to individuals seeking employment or career advancement. These agencies may offer workshops, job listings, and vocational training programs.
- Nonprofit Organizations: Nonprofit organizations focused on workforce development or career readiness may offer career counseling services to individuals in need, including veterans, immigrants, and individuals facing barriers to employment. These organizations may provide job coaching, skills training, and support services.
- Online Platforms: There are various online platforms and resources where individuals can access virtual career counseling services and resources. These platforms may offer career assessments, webinars, articles, and forums where individuals can seek advice and support from career experts.
- Professional Associations: Industry-specific professional associations often provide career development resources and networking opportunities to their members. Career advisors within these associations may offer guidance on career advancement, professional development opportunities, and industry trends.

A Roadmap for Starting a New Hobby or Extracurricular Activity

1. Starting a new hobby or extracurricular activity can be an exciting journey of self-discovery and personal growth. Here's a roadmap to help you get started:

2. Explore Your Interests: Begin by reflecting on your interests, passions, and curiosities. Consider activities you've always wanted to try or subjects that pique your curiosity. Think about what brings you joy and fulfillment. You can explore potential hobbies by browsing online, visiting local hobby shops, attending community events, or asking friends and family for recommendations.

3. Research: Once you've identified a few potential hobbies or activities, take some time to research them further. Look into what each hobby entails, what skills or supplies are needed, and what the learning curve might be like. Explore online tutorials, books, or classes related to your chosen activity to gain a better understanding of what to expect.

4. Gather Necessary Supplies: Depending on the hobby or activity you've chosen, you may need specific supplies or equipment to get started. Make a list of the essential items you'll need and gather them together. This might include art supplies for painting or drawing, musical instruments for learning to play music, gardening tools, or sports equipment for engaging in physical activities. Consider borrowing or renting equipment initially to see if you enjoy the hobby before investing in expensive items.

5. Set Goals and Timeframes: Establishing clear goals and timeframes can help you stay motivated and focused as you embark on your new hobby or activity. Think about what you hope to achieve through your hobby, whether it's

mastering a new skill, creating something meaningful, or simply enjoying the process. Break down your goals into smaller, achievable milestones, and set deadlines or timeframes for reaching them. For example, if you're learning to play a musical instrument, your goals might include mastering a particular song within a month or improving your technique by practicing for a certain number of hours each week.

6. Create a Schedule: Incorporate your new hobby into your regular routine by creating a schedule or timetable. Allocate dedicated time slots for practicing or engaging in your chosen activity, and stick to them as much as possible. Consistency is key to making progress and seeing results in any hobby or pursuit. Consider setting aside specific days or times each week to devote to your hobby, and treat these sessions as non-negotiable appointments with yourself.

7. Stay Flexible and Have Fun: While setting goals and following a schedule can help you make progress in your new hobby, it's essential to remain flexible and adaptable along the way. Embrace the learning process, celebrate your achievements, and don't be afraid to experiment or try new things. Remember that hobbies are meant to be enjoyable and fulfilling, so focus on having fun and exploring your interests without putting too much pressure on yourself to be perfect.

By following this roadmap, you can embark on a rewarding journey of exploration and growth as you discover and cultivate new hobbies and extracurricular activities that bring joy and enrichment to your life.

SUMMING IT UP

Exploring different hobbies and extracurricular activities can be both challenging and rewarding. It's an opportunity to discover new interests, develop valuable skills, and enrich your life in meaningful ways. However, it's essential to remember that not every hobby will be the right fit for you, and that's okay. The journey of exploration is about learning what brings you joy and fulfillment, and sometimes, that means trying out different things until you find the perfect fit.

Having support when trying new things can make the learning process easier and more enjoyable. Whether it's guidance from friends, family members, mentors, or community resources, having a support system can provide encouragement, advice, and motivation along the way. They can offer insights, share experiences, and help you navigate challenges, ultimately enhancing your journey of exploration and growth.

As we transition into the next chapter, "Impacts of Community," we'll explore the role of community in shaping our experiences, providing support, and fostering connections that enrich our lives. From finding like-minded individuals to collaborating on projects and initiatives, community plays a significant role in our personal development and well-being. Let's delve into how community influences our lives and the ways in which we can actively engage with and contribute to our communities for mutual benefit.

IMPACTS OF COMMUNITY

" *Friendship is unnecessary, like philosophy, like art [. . . .] It has no survival value; rather it is one of those things that give value to survival.*

— C.S. LEWIS

Alex and Lily walk down the bustling hallway, engaged in conversation about their upcoming history project. Suddenly, Emily appears, her expression tense as she relays a concerning message.

"Hey, guys," she says urgently, "Natalie just asked me if she could copy my homework for English class."

Concerned, Alex and Lily exchange glances before responding.

"That's not cool," Lily remarks firmly. "You shouldn't let her copy your work. It's not fair to you, and it's not helping her learn anything."

Alex nods in agreement, adding, "Yeah, you don't want to get in trouble for academic dishonesty. Maybe you could offer to tutor her instead so she can understand the material better."

Emily considers their advice, grateful for their support in navigating this ethical dilemma. Then, smiling appreciatively, Emily nods. "You guys are right. Thanks for looking out for me."

As they continue down the hallway, Alex puts a hand on Emily's shoulder.

"Of course, that's what friends are for. We've got each other's backs, no matter what."

Lily chimes in, "Yeah, exactly. We're a team."

With a sense of unity and reassurance, they walk together, knowing they can rely on each other through thick and thin.

* * *

Just as Emily, Alex, and Lily rely on each other for support, having a strong support system is crucial for facing life's challenges. Friends, family, and positive role models like teachers and mentors offer understanding, empathy, and guidance, providing encouragement and perspective during tough times. Having a support network alleviates stress, boosts self-confidence, and fosters resilience, making it easier to navigate academic pressures, peer conflicts, and personal struggles. In this chapter, we'll explore the importance of cultivating these relationships and offer practical tips for building and maintaining a supportive network to help you stand strong under pressure.

SUPPORT NETWORK

Having a strong support system is super important for figuring out who you are, dealing with stress, and bouncing back when things get tough. This is highlighted in *The Secret to Building Resilience* from the Harvard Business Review. According to the article, resilience is not solely an individual characteristic but is heavily influenced by strong relationships and networks. It is facilitated through various interactions with people in both personal and professional spheres. These interactions provide support, empathy, perspective, and motivation to persist through tough times. As the article suggests, "resilience is found not just in having a network of supporters, but in truly connecting with them when you need them most." This connection with support networks helps us navigate challenges by offering validation, different perspectives, and emotional outlets.

Who Is In My Support Network?

- Parents:
  - Role models: Parents serve as role models by demonstrating positive behaviors and values, inspiring their children to emulate them.
  - Advocating: Parents advocate for their children's needs and rights in various settings, such as schools, healthcare, and communities.
  - Emotional support: Parents provide emotional support by listening, empathizing, and offering encouragement during difficult times.
- Teachers:
  - Role models: Teachers act as role models by exemplifying dedication, passion for learning, and integrity in their profession.
  - Advocating: Teachers advocate for their students' academic and personal growth, ensuring they have access to resources and opportunities for success.
  - Mentoring: Teachers mentor students by providing guidance, feedback, and advice to help them navigate academic challenges and career choices.
- Coaches:
  - Role models: Coaches serve as role models by demonstrating discipline, teamwork, and sportsmanship, inspiring athletes to strive for excellence on and off the field.
  - Advocating: Coaches advocate for their athletes' physical and mental well-being, ensuring they have the support and resources needed to succeed in their sport.
  - Emotional support: Coaches provide emotional support by fostering a supportive team environment, building camaraderie, and offering encouragement during both victories and setbacks.
- Aunts/Uncles:
  - Role models: Aunts and uncles can serve as additional role models, offering different perspectives and experiences to enrich their nieces' and nephews' lives.
  - Mentoring: Aunts and uncles can serve as mentors, providing guidance, advice, and support to help their nieces and nephews navigate challenges and make informed decisions.
- Older siblings:
  - Role models: Older siblings can serve as role models by sharing their experiences, offering advice, and setting positive examples for their younger siblings to follow.
  - Emotional support: Older siblings provide emotional support by offering a listening ear, understanding, and empathy during times of stress or uncertainty.

Overall, these supportive adults play crucial roles in providing guidance, encouragement, and empathy, which are essential for people like us who want to develop resilience and thrive in the face of adversity.

UNDER PRESSURE

Navigating high school social situations can be incredibly challenging, as we often grapple with peer pressure and the desire to fit in while staying true to ourselves. The influence of our peers can be both negative and positive, impacting crucial decision-making processes and academic performance. In the article, *How peer pressure does—and doesn't—influence our choices*, Kelly Haws explains that "broadly speaking, we tend to match the choices of others along ordinal lines. These might be numerical characteristics such as size, price, or number, but also more abstract value-based concepts like perceived healthiness, prestige, or authenticity." This highlights how individuals often align their choices with those of their peers, whether consciously or subconsciously, to conform to social norms or gain acceptance within their social circles. However, it's important to recognize that peer pressure isn't always detrimental; positive peer influence can motivate us as students to excel academically, engage in extracurricular activities, and make responsible decisions. Nonetheless, it's crucial for us to develop strong self-awareness and resilience to navigate the complexities of peer pressure and maintain our individuality while navigating the social landscape of high school.

How to Deal with Peer Pressure
• **Set personal boundaries:** Know your values and limits, and stick to them even if others pressure you to do otherwise.
• **Surround yourself with supportive friends:** Choose friends who respect your decisions and encourage you to stay true to yourself.
• **Practice assertiveness:** Communicate your feelings and decisions confidently without being aggressive or passive.
• **Plan ahead:** Anticipate situations where you might face peer pressure and decide in advance how you will respond.
• **Have an exit strategy:** If you find yourself in an uncomfortable situation, know how to gracefully remove yourself from it.
• **Seek adult guidance:** Talk to a trusted adult, like a parent, teacher, or counselor, for advice and support.
• **Focus on your goals:** Keep your long-term goals in mind and remember that succumbing to peer pressure can derail your plans.
• **Be selective:** Choose your social circles wisely and spend time with people who uplift and support you.
• **Practice self-confidence:** Build your self-esteem by engaging in activities you enjoy and celebrating your achievements.
• **Remember that it's okay to say no:** Understand that saying no to peer pressure is a sign of strength, not weakness.

In Chapter 3, we learned how having strong self-esteem is super important. Well, it is even more important here while we talk about peer pressure and being independant. When we believe in ourselves, it's easier to resist things that go against our values. Plus, high self-esteem makes us a positive influence on others. When we're confident and believe in ourselves, we inspire others to do the same. So, by boosting our self-esteem, we not only protect ourselves from bad influences but also become role models for those around us.

BUILT TO LAST

Making and maintaining friendships is super important during our teen years. They give you a sense of belonging and support outside of your family, which can be a big help as you figure out who you are and what you want. As the Raising Children Network says, "Good friends and friendships are important to pre-teens and teenagers because they give them a sense of belonging and being valued by people other than their family." So, it's not just about hanging out; friends help you grow, learn, and have fun along the way. As you navigate these friendships, remember to be kind, supportive, and understanding, and look for friends who do the same for you.

How to Create a Meaningful Relationship

- **Be Authentic:** Show your true self and be genuine in your interactions.
- **Listen Actively:** Pay attention to what others are saying without interrupting, and respond thoughtfully.
- **Be Empathetic:** Try to understand others' perspectives and feelings.
- **Communicate Effectively:** Express yourself clearly and respectfully, and encourage open communication.
- **Show Appreciation:** Acknowledge and thank others for their contributions and support.
- **Spend Quality Time:** Invest time in building and nurturing relationships through meaningful activities and conversations.
- **Be Supportive:** Offer help, encouragement, and emotional support when needed.
- **Respect Boundaries:** Recognize and honor others' personal space, opinions, and boundaries.
- **Stay Connected:** Maintain regular contact and check-ins to show you value the relationship.
- **Resolve Conflicts Constructively:** Address issues calmly, listen to each other's perspectives, and work towards finding solutions together.

SUMMING IT UP

It's clear that relationships and connections are super important in both our personal and professional lives. They're what give us a sense of belonging, support and happiness, while also helping us learn how to work well with others, which is essential for jobs and careers later on. By focusing on building strong friendships and connections now, we're not just making life more enjoyable, but also laying down a foundation for success in the future. In the next chapter, we'll dive into how to start building those important working relationships and making the most out of them.

NAVIGATING NEW EXPERIENCES

66 *Some things cannot be taught; they must be experienced.*
You never learn the most valuable lessons in life until you
go through your own journey.

— ROY T. BENNETT

L ily and Emily are sitting at a cozy corner table in the
bustling coffee shop, sipping their favorite drinks and chat-
ting animatedly.

Suddenly, Alex strides in, looking a bit flustered.

"Hey guys," he greets them, sliding into the seat beside them. "I've
been searching everywhere, but I just can't seem to land a job. I
mean, I have zero experience!"

Lily nods sympathetically, understanding Alex's frustration.

"Yeah, it's tough out there," she acknowledges. "Especially with
everyone looking for experience."

Emily chimes in, her expression thoughtful.

"But you know," she begins, "sometimes it's not just about the experience you have. It's also about how you present yourself and the skills you can offer."

Alex's brow furrows slightly as he considers her words. "What do you mean?" he asks, curiosity piqued.

"Well," Emily continues, "even if you don't have traditional work experience, think about all the other things you've done. Have you ever volunteered, taken on leadership roles in clubs or teams, or even helped out with projects at school? Those are all valuable experiences that demonstrate skills like teamwork, responsibility, and initiative."

Lily nods in agreement. "And don't forget about the skills you've developed outside of formal settings," she adds. "Things like problem-solving, communication, and adaptability are all important in the workplace, too."

Emily leans forward, her eyes alight with enthusiasm. "You know," she begins, "there are so many skills you can develop early on that can really set you up for success in any job."

Lily nods in agreement. "Definitely," she says. "Things like communication skills, time management, and the ability to work well in a team are all crucial."

Alex furrows his brow, considering their words. "But how do you develop those skills if you don't have any work experience?" he asks.

Emily smiles reassuringly. "There are plenty of ways," she says. "Even entry-level jobs, volunteering, and internships can provide valuable opportunities to develop and hone those skills."

Lily nods in agreement. "Absolutely," she says. "Even something as simple as working a part-time job at a store or restaurant can teach you a lot about customer service, problem-solving, and multitasking."

Emily adds, "And don't underestimate the value of volunteering. Whether it's at a local charity, community center, or even within your school, volunteering can help you build connections, develop new skills, and make a positive impact in your community."

Alex's expression brightens as he considers their words. "I never thought about it that way," he admits.

Lily smiles encouragingly. "It's all about taking advantage of the opportunities you have and being willing to learn and grow along the way."

* * *

As Emily, Lily, and Alex gather at the coffee shop, their conversation about finding jobs without experience reflects the common dilemma many teenagers face after college. The uncertainty of post-graduation plans weighs heavily on their minds *daily*. Yet, amidst the challenges lie opportunities. By seeking internships, volunteer roles, and entry-level positions, they can start building the skills needed for their desired careers. Though the road ahead may seem daunting, knowing they're not alone in this journey offers comfort and support as they navigate the path to success together.

EXPERIENCE IS EVERYWHERE

Understanding the struggle of stepping into the job market for the first time is terrifying; let's face it.. It can feel like an uphill battle, with many entry-level positions demanding years of experience, qualifications, and a mix of soft and hard skills. This reality might seem overwhelming, leaving you feeling stuck in a cycle where you need experience to get a job, but you need a job to gain experience. It's a frustrating situation that can make you wonder how to gain experience if no one is willing to give you a chance. But it's important to know you're not alone in facing these challenges. Despite the obstacles, there are ways to break through. Exploring internships, volunteering opportunities, personal projects, or obtaining relevant certifications can showcase your potential and readiness to contribute. Remember, perseverance, resilience, and a proactive mindset are your allies in overcoming the hurdles of the job market as a teenager.

It's totally normal to feel overwhelmed, especially when you see job postings asking for experience you don't yet have.

But here's the thing: *it's okay to start small.*

Don't underestimate the value of gaining experience, even if it's not directly related to your future career goals. Starting with entry-level positions or internships in different industries can actually be a great way to build essential soft skills like communication, teamwork, time management, and problem-solving. These skills are like building blocks you can carry with you throughout your career, no matter where you end up. "But a first job doesn't need to be linked to a future career," says Kate Furey, a career insights specialist at Indeed. "It's about gaining experience, showing that you're reliable, learning how to communicate well with your manager, colleagues, and customers, and getting a sense of what a structured work environment is like."

So, don't be afraid to take on roles that may seem unrelated to your ultimate ambitions. Every experience is an opportunity to learn and grow, and each step, no matter how small, brings you closer to where you want to be.

Building Skills Through Study

Examples of soft skills that can be developed in hospitality or retail positions while gaining hard skills in other areas:

- **Interpersonal Skills:** Interacting with customers and colleagues enhances communication abilities, conflict resolution, and teamwork.
- **Customer Service:** Dealing with various customer needs hones problem-solving skills and teaches patience and empathy.
- **Time Management:** Balancing tasks and responsibilities in fast-paced environments improves organizational skills and efficiency.
- **Adaptability:** Responding to changing situations and customer demands fosters flexibility and resilience.
- **Leadership:** Taking on supervisory roles or guiding new employees develops leadership qualities and delegation skills.
- **Stress Management:** Handling demanding situations and managing multiple tasks simultaneously builds resilience and stress-coping mechanisms.
- **Sales Techniques:** Learning to persuade and influence customers cultivates negotiation skills and enhances persuasive communication.
- **Attention to Detail:** Ensuring accuracy in transactions and product displays sharpens attention to detail and quality standards.
- **Conflict Resolution:** Resolving customer complaints and managing disputes promotes diplomacy and conflict resolution skills.
- **Emotional Intelligence:** Understanding and managing emotions, both yours and others, improves emotional intelligence and interpersonal relationships.

FINDING SATISFACTION AND EXPERIENCE

Volunteering offers a gateway to both personal and professional development, allowing you to expand your skill set while making a positive impact on the world. Beyond just lending a hand, volunteering exposes you to diverse environments, challenges, and people, providing valuable experiences that can shape your future endeavors. By aligning with causes that resonate with your values, you not only contribute to the community but also find deep satisfaction and fulfillment in your actions. So, embrace the opportunity to volunteer, seize the chance to grow, and relish the rewards of giving back to society.

Fortunately, we have the power to make a meaningful impact by volunteering in areas that align with our interests and passions. Here are some inspiring ideas to get started:

When Volunteering Aligns with the Soft Skills We Need

- **Walk dogs for elderly or infirm neighbors:**
  - Responsibility
  - Time management
  - Compassion
- **Visit with elderly or infirm neighbors:**
  - Empathy
  - Communication
  - Patience
- **Prepare or serve meals at a local soup kitchen:**
  - Teamwork
  - Adaptability
  - Empathy
- **Help younger students with homework after school:**
  - Teaching/mentoring
  - Patience
  - Problem-solving
- **Offer to grocery shop for an elderly or infirm person:**
  - Reliability
  - Attention to detail
  - Compassion
- **Assist older individuals with technology:**
  - Communication
  - Problem-solving
  - Adaptability
- **Provide free child care to family members or friends:**
  - Responsibility
  - Patience
  - Adaptability
- **Fundraise for a cause you care about:**
  - Communication
  - Leadership
  - Organization

- **Volunteer at an animal shelter:**
  - Compassion
  - Teamwork
  - Adaptability
- **Hand out socks to the homeless:**
  - Compassion
  - Empathy
  - Communication
- **Send holiday cards to military serving overseas:**
  - Gratitude
  - Empathy
  - Thoughtfulness
- **Gather gently-used books and bring them to a local children's hospital:**
  - Generosity
  - Organization
  - Empathy
- **Volunteer at a local hospital:**
  - Empathy
  - Communication
  - Adaptability
- **Donate old clothes or toys:**
  - Generosity
  - Organization
  - Compassion
- **Handwrite kind notes to strangers and leave them inside books:**
  - Kindness
  - Empathy
  - Creativity
- **Get involved in a community garden:**
  - Teamwork
  - Responsibility
  - Environmental awareness
- **Teach English to immigrants:**
  - Teaching/mentoring
  - Patience
  - Cross-cultural communication
- **Get involved in local politics:**
  - Civic engagement
  - Leadership
  - Communication
- **Coach youth sports:**
  - Leadership
  - Communication
  - Teamwork
- **Offer free music lessons:**
  - Teaching/mentoring
  - Patience
  - Creativity

- **Make dog toys out of old t-shirts and donate them to a local shelter:**
  - Creativity
  - Resourcefulness
  - Compassion
- **Volunteer for a crisis hotline:**
  - Active listening
  - Empathy
  - Crisis management

Visit DoSomething.org for more volunteering opportunities.

By giving back to the community in these ways, we not only develop valuable skills but also experience the satisfaction of making a difference in the lives of others.

INTERNSHIPS

Internships are like real-world boot camps for teens, offering a hands-on experience of what it's like to work in a professional environment. They're not just about making copies or fetching coffee; they're about diving headfirst into the action and gaining valuable skills that can't be taught in a classroom. In the article, *7 Things You'll Learn From Doing an Internship,* Shahira Mohseni explains that,"From researching competitors to crafting marketing plans, I turned my textbook knowledge into practical know-how."

One big perk of internships is the chance to learn hard skills directly related to your interests. Whether it's mastering coding, graphic design, or event planning, internships let you roll up your sleeves and get your hands dirty under the guidance of seasoned pros. It's like having a backstage pass to the industry you're passionate about.

But it's not just about skills; it's also about connections. Internships are golden opportunities to network with professionals in your field. By rubbing elbows with colleagues and supervisors, you can build a web of contacts that might just land you your dream job down the line. As Shahira found, "I learned how to talk shop and make connections with fellow interns and industry pros alike."

In a nutshell, internships are like crash courses in the real world. They give teens a taste of what it's like to work in their chosen field, equip them with valuable skills, and open doors to new opportunities. So, if you're looking to jumpstart your career, an internship might just be the perfect launchpad.

How to Make the Most of Internships

- **Set Clear Goals:** Before starting your internship, outline what you hope to achieve. Whether mastering a specific skill, expanding your network, or gaining insight into a particular industry, having clear objectives will guide your experience.
- **Be Proactive:** Don't wait for tasks to come to you; seek out opportunities to contribute. Volunteer for projects, ask for additional responsibilities and show initiative in your work. Proactivity demonstrates your enthusiasm and dedication.
- **Network Effectively:** Take advantage of networking opportunities within your internship. Connect with colleagues, supervisors, and industry professionals. Attend company events, participate in meetings, and engage in conversations to build meaningful relationships.
- **Seek Feedback:** Actively seek feedback on your performance throughout the internship. Use constructive criticism to improve your skills and address areas for growth. Demonstrating a willingness to learn and adapt will leave a positive impression.
- **Stay Organized:** Keep track of your tasks, deadlines, and accomplishments. Maintain a schedule, prioritize your workload, and meet deadlines consistently. Being organized demonstrates professionalism and reliability.
- **Learn Continuously:** View your internship as a learning experience and embrace opportunities for growth. Ask questions, observe processes, and seek out new knowledge. Be receptive to feedback and actively seek out resources to expand your skills.
- **Build Relationships:** Cultivate relationships with your colleagues and supervisors. Show genuine interest in their work, offer assistance, and demonstrate respect and professionalism. Building strong relationships can lead to valuable mentorship and future opportunities.
- **Reflect Regularly:** Take time to reflect on your experiences and accomplishments during the internship. Consider what you've learned, how you've grown, and areas for improvement. Reflection can help you make the most of your internship experience and prepare you for future endeavors.

SUMMING IT UP

It can't be stressed enough how important it is to get out there and gather experience from different places. It's like building up your toolkit for the future. Whether you're doing an internship, volunteering, or working part-time, each gig teaches you something new and helps you grow.

See, having experience from different spots makes you super flexible. You can handle all kinds of situations, work with different teams, and tackle challenges like a pro. Plus, bosses love seeing that you've got a wide range of skills under your belt.

Bu here's the thing: *life isn't always smooth sailing.*

You're gonna face setbacks, like not getting a job you wanted or feeling like you've failed at something. It's tough, but it's all part of the journey.

The key is to bounce back stronger. Take those tough moments as lessons, learn from them, and keep pushing forward. Embrace the bumps in the road as chances to grow and get better. That way, you'll be ready to tackle whatever comes your way on your path to success.

GOING THE DISTANCE

> *Success is not final, failure is not fatal: it is the courage to continue that counts.*
>
> — WINSTON S. CHURCHILL

Emily and Alex sit quietly in the bustling high school cafeteria, their usual animated conversations replaced by heavy silence. Both wear somber expressions, their eyes fixed on their untouched lunches. The weight of sadness hangs palpably in the air around them, casting a shadow over the vibrant atmosphere of the cafeteria.

As they sit lost in their thoughts, Lily, a compassionate classmate, notices their downcast demeanor from across the room. Concern etches her features as she approaches their table, her footsteps hesitant yet determined.

"Hey, Emily. Hey, Alex," Lily says softly, her voice carrying a gentle tone of concern. "Is everything okay?"

Emily speaks first. "I... I got rejected from my top college," she confesses, her eyes downcast as she speaks. The sting of rejection still fresh, she feels a lump forming in her throat, threatening to choke back her words.

Lily's expression softens with empathy as she reaches out to squeeze Emily's hand in a gesture of comfort. "I'm so sorry, Emily. That must be really tough," she offers, her voice filled with genuine sympathy.

Beside her, Alex shifts uncomfortably in his seat, his own struggle weighing heavily on his mind. With a heavy sigh, he decides to share his own disappointment with the group.

"Yeah, and I... I didn't get the sports scholarship I was hoping for," Alex admits, his voice tinged with a hint of frustration. With the dream of playing at the collegiate level slipping through his fingers, he feels a pang of regret gnawing at his insides.

Lily's heart goes out to her friends as she listens to their admissions, her empathy guiding her response. "I know it may not feel like it right now, but rejection is not a reflection of your worth," she reassures them, her voice filled with sincerity. "You both have worked so hard, and setbacks like these are just temporary roadblocks on your journey to success."

However, neither friend was comforted by Lily's words, so she tried again. "Have you ever heard of that quote by Winston Churchill?"

"Which one?" Alex asks.

"You know, the one where he says, 'success is not final, failure is not fatal: it is the courage to continue that counts.'"

"*Oh,* that one." Reflecting on the profound meaning behind the quote, Emily shares her thoughts. "I think I know where you're going with that. It's easy to get caught up in the fear of failure or the fleeting euphoria of success," she muses, "but what really matters is having the courage to persevere, no matter the outcome."

Alex sighs. "You do have a point. I guess that failure doesn't define us," he adds. "It's how we respond to it that shapes our character and defines our journey."

Lily chimes in, her voice tinged with optimism. "Sometimes, it takes courage just to keep going, especially when faced with setbacks or disappointments," she says. "But that's where true strength lies - in our ability to rise above adversity and continue moving forward."

"Handling rejection isn't easy," Lily admits, "but it's essential to remember that a setback doesn't define your worth or your future. It's merely a stepping stone on your journey to success."

Emily nods in agreement, recognizing the importance of positive self-talk and the ability to pivot in the face of disappointment. "It's all about finding meaning in the work you do," she reflects, "and not letting setbacks derail your sense of purpose."

Alex chimes in, sharing his own experiences of dealing with failure and emphasizing the role of adaptability in navigating life's twists and turns. "Change is inevitable," he remarks, "but it's how we respond to it that truly matters. Embracing change opens up new opportunities for growth and fulfillment."

Their conversation then turns to the diverse definitions of success, prompting them to reflect on their own values and aspirations. They discuss examples ranging from wealth and satisfaction to philanthropy and community, realizing that success is a deeply personal concept shaped by individual values and goals.

As they wrap up their conversation, Lily offers a reassuring reminder to her friends: "Finding your path in life may not always be straightforward, but as long as you stay true to yourself and pursue what truly matters to you, you'll find satisfaction and purpose along the way."

With a renewed sense of hope and determination, Emily, Alex, and Lily leave the cafeteria, ready to face whatever challenges lie ahead on their journey toward success.

* * *

Emily, Alex, and Lily find themselves facing setbacks and feeling alone in their struggles. We all do, don't we? The thing is, they understand that it's not about avoiding failure but about how they respond to it. They talk about the importance of resilience and determination in pursuing their dreams, even when challenges arise. In this chapter, we will explore the ups and downs of committing to a career, knowing that even dream jobs can have setbacks. You will learn tips for finding joy in your work and bouncing back from failure. Through their conversation, Emily, Alex, and Lily realize they're not alone. They're inspired to keep pushing forward, knowing that with resilience and determination, they can overcome any obstacle on their path to success. And *you* can, too.

PLANNING FOR FAILURE

Rejection and failure are like the unwelcome guests at life's never-ending party. Seriously! They always seem to show up, whether we want them to or not. But here's the thing: they're not just party crashers; they're actually pretty important for our growth, just like that cheesy line from Henry Ford:

Failure is simply the opportunity to begin again, this time more intelligently.

Humans are bound to encounter setbacks, make mistakes, and face rejection at various points in their careers. However, it is how they respond to these challenges that ultimately defines their leadership abilities.

So, picture this: you're cruising through life, doing your thing, and suddenly, bam! You hit a roadblock. Maybe you didn't get that scholarship you wanted, or your big project at school totally flopped. It *stings*, right? But here's the silver lining… failure is like a crash course in personal development. As Dr. Slover explains, "The reason why failure is important in leadership is because it allows the leader to define themselves by new learning, rather than by the failure." Failure forces you to take a step back, reassess your approach, and figure out what went wrong.

Think about it this way: failure isn't just about falling flat on your face; it's about getting back up, dusting yourself off, and figuring out how to do better next time. It's like those video game bosses that seem impossible to beat at first, but once you figure out their weak spot, they're toast.

And here's another cool thing about failure: it's a great teacher. When things go south, it's a chance to learn from your mistakes, grow from your experiences, and come back stronger than ever. Plus, it's a reminder that nobody – not even the coolest, most successful leaders out there – have it all figured out.

So yeah, rejection and failure might suck in the moment, but trust me, they're not the end of the world. In fact, they're just the beginning of something new and even better. So next time you face a setback, remember: it's not about how hard you fall, but how high you bounce back.

How to Turn Your Failure... Into an Opportunity	
Example Scenario	Example Opportunities to Grow
Rejection from your top-choice college or university.	Use it as motivation to explore other options and find the best fit for your academic and personal goals. It's a chance to broaden your horizons and discover new opportunities.
Not receiving a scholarship you applied for.	View it as an opportunity to develop resilience and resourcefulness. Look for alternative funding sources, such as grants, part-time work, or financial aid programs.
Failing an important exam or class.	See it as a learning experience rather than a reflection of your abilities. Identify areas for improvement, seek help from teachers or tutors, and develop effective study habits for future success.
Being turned down for a job or internship opportunity.	Use it as an opportunity to refine your resume, cover letter, and interview skills. Seek feedback from professionals in your field of interest and continue to pursue relevant experiences and opportunities.
Receiving negative feedback on a project or presentation.	Embrace it as constructive criticism that can help you grow and improve. Reflect on the feedback, identify areas for enhancement, and use it to refine your skills and approaches in future projects.
Not getting elected for a leadership position in a school club or organization.	View it as an opportunity to develop humility and teamwork skills. Stay involved in the organization, support the elected leaders, and look for other ways to contribute and make a positive impact.
Facing difficulties balancing academics and extracurricular activities.	See it as an opportunity to develop time management and prioritization skills. Explore strategies for better organization, seek support from teachers and mentors, and remember to prioritize self-care and well-being.
Facing interpersonal conflicts or misunderstandings with friends	See it as an opportunity to practice communication and conflict resolution skills. Take a step back to reflect on the situation and consider the perspectives of others involved. Approach the conversation with empathy, active listening, and a willingness to compromise. Focus on finding common ground and resolving the issue constructively rather than placing blame or escalating the conflict. Strengthening friendships through honest communication can lead to greater trust and understanding in the long run.
Experiencing setbacks in personal relationships or family dynamics	See it as an opportunity to strengthen communication and interpersonal skills. Practice active listening, empathy, and conflict resolution techniques to constructively navigate challenging conversations and conflicts. Seek support from trusted friends, family members, or counselors for guidance and perspective. Set boundaries and prioritize self-care to maintain emotional well-being and resilience in difficult situations. Focus on building and nurturing healthy relationships based on mutual respect, trust, and understanding.

When faced with failure, it's important to give yourself permission to feel all the emotions that come with it. It's normal to feel disappointed, sad, or even angry. The University of Melbourne's article, "Coping with Failure" advises that instead of trying to push those feelings away, let yourself experience them. They say you should "give yourself permission to feel... allow yourself time to experience it, remembering that failure is a part of everyone's life experience, and actually crucial to success." Remember, everyone fails sometimes. Be kind to yourself during this time. Treat yourself with the same compassion you would offer a friend who is going through a tough time. Embrace a growth mindset where you see failure as an opportunity to learn and grow. Reflect on what went wrong and think about how you can do things differently next time. Finally, don't let failure hold you back. Take the time to reassess your goals and make a plan for the future. Make sure your goals are realistic and align with what's important to you. By approaching failure with resilience and a positive attitude, you can turn setbacks into stepping stones toward your dreams.

NOT ALL SUCCESS IS THE SAME

When things don't go as planned, it can feel pretty overwhelming, right?

But here's the thing: failure and change aren't always bad. In fact, they can lead us to discover our true passions and purpose in life. Yale's article, "Learn and Grow: What is adaptability in the workplace?" explains that "Change is a natural part of life; therefore, adaptability is a crucial skill. When we accept that nothing stays the same forever, it gives us room to look for new opportunities to grow personally and professionally. Fighting change that you truly have no control over is like trying to keep the sun from rising or setting. Being actively involved helps you to embrace change by understanding it, being receptive, open, and adaptable."

You heard it right... change is just a part of life. It happens whether we like it or not. And being able to adapt and go with the flow is a really important skill.

Instead of resisting change, let's welcome it with open arms. Change isn't always easy, but it's a chance for us to evolve and discover new aspects of ourselves. When we embrace change, we open ourselves up to growth and learning opportunities that can ultimately make us stronger individuals. Think of it like a tree bending in the wind... it may sway and bend, but it remains rooted and resilient. By staying open-minded and adaptable, we can navigate through life's twists and turns with grace and determination, emerging stronger and more resilient in the end. So, let's embrace change as a natural part of life's journey and use it as a catalyst for personal growth and development.

Our Success = Our Values

Let's take a step back and revisit Chapter 1, where we talked about what success means to each of us. It's worth digging into again because it's a fundamental aspect of our journey. Success isn't just hitting some grand milestone or amassing wealth. It's about living a life that feels right to you, one that resonates with your values.

Think about what really matters to you. Is it about making a positive impact on others? Following your passions? Your values are like your North Star, guiding you toward what's truly important in life. Let's say you're all about making a difference in the world. You might thrive in a career in social work or environmental activism, where you can directly contribute to causes you believe in. Or, if pursuing your passions is your thing, diving into a career in music or filmmaking could be your jam, letting you express yourself while making a living. By understanding your values and what drives you, you can carve out a path that not only makes you happy but also leaves a mark on the world.

So, it's valuable to pause and reflect on your values and how they shape your vision of success. Once you've got a handle on that, you'll have a clearer direction for your journey ahead. And that's where the real magic happens.

Take a Moment to Think: What Does Success Mean to You?

Success isn't a one-size-fits-all concept. It's deeply personal and unique to each individual. For some, it might be reaching a specific career milestone, while for others, it could be nurturing meaningful relationships or making a positive impact in their community.

Consider what brings you fulfillment and satisfaction. Is it achieving your goals, no matter how big or small? Or perhaps it's about finding balance and contentment in your daily life.

Your definition of success is a compass that guides your choices and actions. So, take the time to explore what truly matters to you and let that shape your path forward. After all, success isn't just about reaching the destination… it's about enjoying the journey along the way.

Look At Your Values for A Glimpse Into Success	
What Do You Value?	What Can Success Look Like to You?
Wealth	For someone who values wealth, success may mean living a lavish lifestyle filled with travel and luxury experiences. They might see success as achieving financial independence through successful entrepreneurial endeavors, allowing them to enjoy the finer things in life without worrying about money.
Satisfaction	Individuals who prioritize satisfaction may define success as accomplishing challenging goals that bring them a sense of fulfillment. This could involve making significant contributions to fields like space exploration or medicine, where their work positively impacts society and leaves a lasting legacy.
Philanthropy	Those who value philanthropy may view success as the ability to make a meaningful difference in the lives of others. They may measure success by their impact on the community, such as providing aid to those in need through charity work or supporting causes they are passionate about.
Community	Success for individuals who prioritize community may revolve around building and nurturing close relationships with loved ones. They may find fulfillment in creating a strong support network and fostering connections within their community, prioritizing quality time spent with family and friends over material possessions or career achievements.
Creativity	For those who value creativity, success may be defined as the ability to express oneself artistically and innovatively. This could involve creating original works of art, music, literature, or contributing groundbreaking ideas to their field of expertise.
Health and Wellness	Individuals prioritizing health and wellness may see success as achieving optimal physical and mental well-being. Success, in this context, could mean maintaining a balanced lifestyle, prioritizing self-care practices, and overcoming personal health challenges to live a fulfilling and vibrant life.
Integrity	For those who value integrity, success is closely tied to maintaining honesty, ethics, and moral principles in all aspects of life. This could mean achieving success in a career where they can uphold their values, such as law, advocacy, or ethical business leadership.
Compassion	For someone who values compassion, success may be defined by the positive impact they make on others' lives. This could involve working in fields like healthcare, social work, or humanitarian aid, where they can directly contribute to improving the well-being of others.

Education and Lifelong Learning	Success for individuals who value education and lifelong learning may involve continuous personal and intellectual growth. This could mean acquiring new knowledge, mastering skills, and pursuing higher levels of education to expand their understanding of the world and reach their full potential.
Adventure and Exploration	Those who prioritize adventure and exploration may define success as experiencing new cultures, pushing personal boundaries, and embracing life's adventures. Success, in this context, could involve embarking on daring expeditions, traveling to exotic destinations, and seeking out thrilling experiences that enrich their lives.
Spirituality and Inner Peace	Success for individuals who value spirituality and inner peace may be centered around finding harmony and connection with their inner selves and the universe. This could involve practicing mindfulness, meditation, and self-reflection to cultivate a sense of serenity, purpose, and spiritual fulfillment.
Inclusivity	For individuals who prioritize inclusivity, success may be defined by their efforts to promote diversity, equity, and inclusion in all aspects of society. This could involve working in diversity and inclusion consulting, education, advocacy, or community organizing to create more equitable and inclusive environments for everyone.
Environment alism	Individuals who prioritize environmentalism may define success by their contributions to sustainability and conservation efforts. Success could involve working in environmental science, renewable energy, conservation organizations, or sustainable business practices to protect the planet and its resources.

SUMMING IT UP

 You build on failure. You use it as a stepping stone. Close the door on the past. You don't try to forget the mistakes, but you don't dwell on it. You don't let it have any of your energy, or any of your time, or any of your space.

— JOHNNY CASH

Finding your dream career might not be like following a straight line on a map. It's more like taking a road trip with some detours and unexpected stops along the way. And guess what? That's totally okay!

Sometimes, you might think you've found the perfect path, only to realize it's not quite right for you. That's normal! It's all about exploring different options and figuring out what truly lights you up inside.

So, don't stress if things don't go according to plan right away. Keep trying new things, taking risks, and following your passions. As long as you're staying true to yourself and what you believe in, you'll find your way to a career that brings you satisfaction and purpose.

Just remember, it's about more than just the destination but the journey itself. So, embrace the twists and turns, learn from all of them, and keep moving forward with confidence.

You've got this!

BE AN INSPIRATION!

The secret to shaping the future you want to have is to be proactive, and with the skills and wisdom you've picked up here, you're well on the road to success. Take a moment now to inspire other young people to take the same journey.

Simply by sharing your honest opinion of this book and a little about what you've found here, you'll help get this information out to more of the teenagers who are looking for it.

Thank you so much for your support. You have a bright future ahead of you. Now go out there and grab it!

Scan the QR code to leave your review or follow the link:

amazon.com/review/create-review?&asin=B0D1WT5BX5

CONCLUSION

— E.E. CUMMINGS

On their high school graduation day, Alex, Emily, and Lily gather together, adorned in their caps and gowns, buzzing with excitement and nerves about the future. Lily, always the optimist, breaks the tension with a reassuring smile.

"You know what?" Lily says, her eyes shining with anticipation. "One day, we'll look back at all this and laugh at how stressed we once were about our future."

Emily nods, a hint of relief evident in her expression. "I know you're right. Looking back, I remember thinking that everything's riding on this moment."

"I remember feeling so intimidated and overwhelmed by the sheer number of career choices out there," Alex confesses, his brow furrowing with the memory. "I just didn't know where to begin."

Lily nods sympathetically. "Yeah, I felt the same way. It was like, how are we supposed to know what we want to do for the rest of our lives when we barely understand our own needs and wants."

Alex sighs, running a hand through his hair. "And then there's the pressure to choose a career that aligns with our values. We don't want to compromise who we are, but sometimes it feels like we have to in order to please others."

The trio exchanges knowing looks, each understanding the weight of these concerns all too well.

"You know," Alex begins, breaking the heavy silence that lingers among them, "despite all the stress and uncertainty, I think we've actually learned a lot over the years."

Emily nods in agreement. "Definitely. I mean, sure, we may not have everything figured out just yet, but we've gained so much knowledge and experience that we can carry with us into the future."

Lily smiles, a sense of optimism creeping into her expression. "Yeah, and I think that's something to be proud of. We may not have all the answers, but we've learned how to navigate challenges and overcome obstacles... and that's a skill that will serve us well in whatever path we choose."

As they bask in the realization of their growth and resilience, a sense of reassurance washes over them. They may not have all the answers, but they have the confidence and determination to face whatever comes their way with courage and resilience.

"And you know what?" Alex adds, determination in his voice. "I truly believe that with everything we've learned, we have the power to create happy and successful lives for ourselves, no matter what challenges may come our way."

TAKE THESE IDEAS WITH YOU

Throughout this book, we've been on a journey of self-discovery, exploring our values, interests, and skills and figuring out what we want in our careers. Here's what we've learned:

Throughout our journey, we've taken the time to really understand ourselves - our values, interests, and skills that we want to bring into our future careers. We've delved into various industries and job roles, broadening our horizons and giving ourselves a clearer idea of the possibilities out there.

But it's not just about landing a job; it's also about taking care of ourselves along the way. We've realized the importance of self-esteem and self-care, recognizing that our time in school is vital for honing our self-management skills, which will set us up for success beyond graduation.

And let's not overlook the significance of our extracurricular activities! They've been more than just a way to pass the time; they've been instrumental in helping us discover our passions and develop valuable skills that will serve us well in the future.

Throughout this journey, our meaningful relationships have been our pillars of support. We've learned the importance of building and nurturing connections with others, as they provide us with the motivation and encouragement we need to keep moving forward.

But it's not just about what we know; it's also about what we do. We've actively sought out opportunities to gain experience in our fields of interest through internships and volunteering, allowing us to refine our skills and gain insight into what our future careers might entail.

And finally, we've spent time reflecting on what success really means to each of us. We understand that it's not always going to be smooth sailing, but we're ready to persevere through challenges and obstacles to achieve our goals.

The best time to start building your future is now. Pursue your interests, set goals, and bring your dream career to life! Embrace the challenges, celebrate the victories, and never lose sight of what truly matters to you. With determination and resilience, you can turn your aspirations into reality. So, take that first step today and let your journey begin!

REFERENCES

"7 Things You'll Learn from Doing an Internship - University of Wollongong." UOW, www.uow.edu.au/study/high-school/7-things-youll-learn-from-doing-an-internship/. Accessed 27 Feb. 2024.

"11 Active Listening Skills to Practice (with Examples) - Indeed." Indeed, www.indeed.com/career-advice/career-development/active-listening-skills. Accessed 1 Feb. 2024.

"24 Volunteer Ideas for Teens." YMCA, www.ymca.org/blog/articles/24-volunteer-ideas-for-teens. Accessed 27 Feb. 2024.

Amitabh, Utkarsh. "The Right Way to Make a Big Career Transition." Harvard Business Review, 11 Oct. 2021, hbr.org/2021/07/the-right-way-to-make-a-big-career-transition.

"Artistic." University College Academic and Career Development, acd.iupui.edu/careers/choose-your-major/connect-majors-to-careers/interests/artistic/index.html. Accessed 3 Feb. 2024.

"Being an Advocate for Your Child." Raising Children Network, 8 Sept. 2021, raisingchildren.net.au/school-age/school-learning/working-with-schools-teachers/being-an-advocate.

"Careers That Fit Your Interests." JCU Australia, 3 Feb. 2023, www.jcu.edu.au/employability-edge/you-and-your-career/careers-that-fit-your-interests.

Davis, Bill. Member, UAGC Staff. "The Value of Purpose, Passion, and Vision, and How to Achieve Success." UAGC, www.uagc.edu/blog/the-value-of-purpose-passion-and-vision-and-how-to-achieve-success. Accessed 1 Feb. 2024.

Dennison, Kara. "How to Have an Authentic Job Search to Find a Company That Aligns with Your Values." Forbes, Forbes Magazine, 25 Apr. 2023, www.forbes.com/sites/karadennison/2023/04/24/how-to-have-an-authentic-job-search-to-find-a-company-that-aligns-with-your-values/?sh=55caf1c069f5.

Dr. Susan Woolford. "Two-thirds of Parents Say Teens and Preteens Are Worried About How They Look." TODAY.Com, TODAY, 20 Sept. 2022, www.today.com/health/mind-body/majority-teens-preteens-self-conscious-appearance-poll-suggests-rcna48492.

Entman, Liz. "How Peer Pressure Does-and Doesn't-Influence Our Choices." Vanderbilt University, Vanderbilt University, 27 Aug. 1970, news.vanderbilt.edu/2019/08/27/how-peer-pressure-does-and-doesnt-influence-our-choices/.

"Finding a Job When You Have No Experience." Harvard Business Review, 1 Sept. 2023, hbr.org/2023/09/finding-a-job-when-you-have-no-experience.

"Free Personality Test, Type Descriptions, Relationship and Career Advice." 16Personalities, www.16personalities.com/. Accessed 3 Feb. 2024.

"Fueling Young People to Change the World." Fueling Young People to Change the World | DoSomething.Org, www.dosomething.org/us. Accessed 27 Feb. 2024.

GCU Blog. "Why Failure Is Important in Leadership." Grand Canyon University, www.gcu.edu/blog/business-management/why-failure-important-leadership.

Goodreads. "Success is not final, failure is not fatal: it is the courage to continue that counts." Goodreads, www.goodreads.com/quotes/3270-success-is-not-final-failure-is-not-fatal-it-is.

Gorodnichenko , Yuriy, and Gerard Roland . Individualism, Innovation, and Long-Run Growth | Proceedings Of ..., www.pnas.org/doi/10.1073/pnas.1101933108. Accessed 12 Feb. 2024.

"Gen Z Research Snapshot: Gen Z Feels Deeply Connected to Social Causes." ASA.Org, American Student Assistance, 1 Nov. 2022, www.asa.org/research/gen-z-research-snapshot-gen-z-feels-deeply-connected-to-social-causes/.

"How to Find a Hobby as an Adult, According to Experts & Women Who've Done It." Bustle, www.bustle.com/wellness/how-to-find-hobby-adult. Accessed 17 Feb. 2024.

Huntington, Charlie. "Passion: Definition, Examples, & Projects." The Berkeley Well-Being Institute, www.berkeleywellbeing.com/passion.html. Accessed 1 Feb. 2024.

Indeed Editorial Team. "Hard Skills vs. Soft Skills | Indeed.Com Australia." Indeed, au.indeed.com/career-advice/resumes-cover-letters/hard-skills-vs-soft-skills. Accessed 2 Feb. 2024.

Indeed Editorial Team. "How to Identify Your Career Interest (with Examples) - Indeed." Indeed, ca.indeed.com/career-advice/career-development/how-to-identify-your-career-interest. Accessed 4 Feb. 2024.

Jill Suttie. "How to Make the Lasting Friendships You Want." Greater Good, greatergood.berkeley.edu/article/item/how_to_make_the_lasting_friendships_you_want. Accessed 27 Feb. 2024.

Ledesma, Cecilio Blanco. "Passion Is a Feeling That Follows Action." Medium, Medium, 14 July 2023, medium.com/@cecilledesma_20547/passion-is-a-feeling-that-follows-action-1098cd87ca9f.

Martin. "48 Positive Affirmations for Kids." Cosmic Kids, 23 Nov. 2023, cosmickids.com/positive-affirmations-for-kids/.

Mentoring Basics - A Mentor's Guide to Success, www.bc.edu/content/dam/files/centers/cwf/individuals/pdf/MentorGuide.pdf. Accessed 27 Feb. 2024.

Mindfulness for Students | Greater Good in Education, ggie.berkeley.edu/student-well-being/mindfulness-for-students/. Accessed 12 Feb. 2024.

"NASA Careers: Frequently Asked Questions." NASA, NASA, 2 Jan. 2024, www.nasa.gov/careers/faq/#I-am-a-student-considering-a-future-career-at-NASA.-What-courses-should-I-take?-What-major-should-I-choose?

Parris, Emilly. "How to Choose a Career Path." Your Guide to Choosing a Career Path: Tips & Advice, Upskilled, www.upskilled.edu.au/skillstalk/how-to-choose-a-career-path. Accessed 3 Feb. 2024.

"Personality Type and Careers." MBTI Type and Career-Find Your Best Work, Myers & Briggs Foundation, 20 July 2023, www.myersbriggs.org/type-in-my-life/personality-type-and-careers/.

Phillips, —Dr. Katherine W. et al. "How Diversity Makes Us Smarter." Greater Good, greatergood.berkeley.edu/article/item/how_diversity_makes_us_smarter. Accessed 12 Feb. 2024.

Self-Discipline | English Meaning - Cambridge Dictionary, dictionary.cambridge.org/dictionary/english/self-discipline. Accessed 17 Feb. 2024.

"Self-Esteem and Self-Confidence." My.UQ, 25 Nov. 2019, my.uq.edu.au/information-and-services/student-support/health-and-wellbeing/self-help-resources/self-esteem-and-self-confidence.

Smillie, Luke D. "How Personality Tests Might Help You Find a Job You'll Love." Psychology Today, Sussex Publishers, www.psychologytoday.com/au/blog/the-patterns-of-persons/202209/how-personality-tests-might-help-you-find-a-job-youll-love. Accessed 3 Feb. 2024.

"Soft Skills and Hard Skills: What's the Difference?" Professional Practice Credentials, Deakin University, 3 June 2019, credentials.deakin.edu.au/soft-skills-and-hard-skills-whats-the-difference/.

Thakuria, Pansy. "50 Dream Job Quotes to Inspire You." Vantage Lens. Last modified March 12, 2024. https://www.vantagelens.com/blog/dream-job-quotes/

"The Secret to Building Resilience." Harvard Business Review, 17 Sept. 2021, hbr.org/2021/01/the-secret-to-building-resilience.

Ulrich Orth. "Is High Self-Esteem Beneficial? Revisiting a Classic Question." Apa PsycNet, American Psychological Association, psycnet.apa.org/fulltext/2022-48842-002.html. Accessed 12 Feb. 2024.

University, Deakin. "How to Choose Your Future Career." Deakin University Australia, www.deakin.edu.au/articles/career/how-to-choose-your-future-career. Accessed 3 Feb. 2024.

University of Melbourne. "Coping with Failure." Counselling & Psychological Services, University of Melbourne, services.unimelb.edu.au/counsel/resources/study-related-issues/coping-with-failure.

"Values." Ethics Unwrapped, 5 Nov. 2022, ethicsunwrapped.utexas.edu/glossary/values.

"Values, Passion, or Purpose - Which Should Guide Your Career?" Harvard Business Review, 26 Oct. 2023, hbr.org/2023/10/values-passion-or-purpose-which-should-guide-your-career.

"What Is Cognitive Dissonance?" Cleveland Clinic, Cleveland Clinic, 22 Dec. 2023, health.clevelandclinic.org/cognitive-dissonance.

"What Is Friendship?" Geneva College, www.geneva.edu/academics/crossroads/geneva-question/what-is-friendship#:~:text=As%20the%20ubiquitous%20C.S.,that%20give%20value%20to%20survival.%E2%80%9D. Accessed 27 Feb. 2024.

White, Sue. "Landing Your First Job: Tips and Tricks for Starters." The Sydney Morning Herald, The Sydney Morning Herald, 25 July 2022, www.smh.com.au/business/workplace/landing-your-first-job-tips-and-tricks-for-starters-20220629-p5axor.html.

Why Is Time Management Important? And How to Manage Your Time | ..., ca.indeed.com/career-advice/career-development/why-is-time-management-important. Accessed 17 Feb. 2024.

Printed in Great Britain
by Amazon

59523693R00079